Berlitz

dip in

Spanish

1000
everyday words and phrases

Berlitz Publishing

New York   London   Singapore

Contacting the Editors
Every effort has been made to provide accurate information in this publication, but changes are inevitable. The publisher cannot be responsible for any resulting loss, inconvenience or injury. We would appreciate it if readers would call our attention to any errors or outdated information. We also welcome your suggestions, please contact us at:
comments@berlitzpublishing.com

First Printing: March 2012
Printed in China

Publishing Director: Mina Patria
Commissioning Editor: Kate Drynan
Editorial Assistant: Sophie Cooper
Cover Design: Beverley Speight
Interior Design: Beverley Speight
Production Manager: Raj Trivedi
Cover Illustration: © Beverley Speight

Contents

1000
everyday words and phrases

Introduction

dip into **Spanish** is intended to help you learn some of the most important words and phrases used in everyday Spanish. In mastering these 1,000 words or so, you will be able to converse and get by reading in up to 80% of situations common to daily life. This book can be used as a study aid, as a quick-reference guide on the go or as the basis for learning new vocabulary from scratch. Although this is not a grammar book, it does contain tips on sentence structure and other cultural facts, spread evenly throughout the sections to enable you to learn more effectively. Each word and phrase is set into context with a sample sentence so you know when and how to use it, and the simplified phonetics will guide you through any tricky pronunciations.

With over 400 million Spanish speakers worldwide, Spanish is the third most widely spoken language in the world and the official language of 21 different nations. Over 17 million people in the United States speak Spanish as their native language, and it is one of the official languages of the United Nations. Spanish is the fourth most popular language on the internet, behind English, Japanese and German. Below are estimated numbers of Spanish speakers around the globe.

Central America: 55 million
North America: 112 million
South America: 190 million
Spain: 40 million

Key

adj	adjective	**m**	masculine
adv	adverb	**pl**	plural
abbr	abbreviation	**pron**	pronoun
art	article	**n**	noun
conj	conjunction	**prep**	preposition
f	feminine	**v**	verb

Pronunciation

This section is designed to make you familiar with the sounds of Spanish using our simplified phonetic transcription. You'll find the pronunciation of the Spanish letters and sounds explained below, together with their 'imitated' equivalents. This system is used throughout the book; simply read the pronunciation as if it were English, noting any special rules indicated below.

Underlined letters indicate that that syllable should be stressed. The acute accent ´ indicates stress, e.g. **río**, *ree•oh*. Some Spanish words have more than one meaning. In these instances, the accent mark is also used to distinguish between them, e.g.: **él** (he) and **el** (the); **sí** (yes) and **si** (if). There are some differences in vocabulary and pronunciation between the Spanish spoken in Spain and that in the Americas — although each is easily understood by the other. This book is specifically geared to travelers in Spain.

Consonants

Letter	Approximate Pronunciation	Symbol	Example	Pronunciation
b	1. as in English	**b**	**bueno**	*bweh•noh*
	2. between vowels as in English, but softer	**b**	**bebida**	*beh•bee•dah*
c	1. before e and i like th in thin	**th**	**centro**	*thehn•troh*
	2. otherwise like k in kit	**k**	**como**	*koh•moh*
ch	as in English	**ch**	**mucho**	*moo•choh*

Letter	Approximate Pronunciation	Symbol	Example	Pronunciation
d	1. as in English	d	donde	_dohn_•deh
	2. between vowels and especially at the end of a word, like th in thin, but softer	th	usted	oos•_teth_
g	1. before e and i, like ch in Scottish loch	kh	urgente	oor•_khehn_•teh
	2. otherwise, like g in get	g	ninguno	neen•_goo_•noh
h	always silent		hombre	ohm•breh
j	like ch in Scottish loch	kh	bajo	_bah_•khoh
ll	like y in yellow	y	lleno	_yeh_•noh
ñ	like ni in onion	ny	señor	seh•_nyohr_
q	like k in kick	k	quince	_keen_•theh
r	trilled, especially at the beginning of a word	r	río	_ree_•oh
rr	strongly trilled	rr	arriba	ah•_rree_•bah
s	1. like s in same	s	sus	soos
	2. before b, d, g, l, m, n, like s in rose	z	mismo	_meez_•moh
v	like b in bad, but softer	b	viejo	_beeyeh_•khoh
z	like th in thin	th	brazo	brah•thoh

Letters f, k, l, m, n, p, t, w, x and y are pronounced as in English.

Vowels

Letter	Approximate Pronunciation	Symbol	Example	Pronunciation
a	like the a in father	**ah**	**gracias**	*grah•theeyahs*
e	like e in get	**eh**	**esta**	*ehs•tah*
i	like ee in meet	**ee**	**sí**	*see*
o	like o in rope	**oh**	**dos**	*dohs*
u	1. like oo in food	**oo**	**uno**	<u>*oo*</u>*•noh*
	2. silent after g and q		**que**	*keh*
	3. when marked like we in well	**w**	**antigüedad**	*ahn•tee•gweh•ü,* <u>*dahd*</u>
y	1. like y in yellow	**y**	**hoy**	*oy*
	2. when alone, like ee in meet	**ee**	**y**	<u>*ee*</u>
	3. when preceded by an a, sounds like y + ee, with ee faintly pronounced	**aye**	**hay**	*aye*

Exclamation & Question Marks

In Spanish, inverted exclamation and question marks are also placed at the beginning of the sentence. This has no effect on the pronunciation and is purely stylistic.

Feedback

Help us to make sure this remains the right book for you by submitting your suggestions to:

comments@berlitzpublishing.com

Alternatively, please write to:

**Berlitz Publishing,
APA Publications Ltd.,
58 Borough High Street,
London SE1 1XF,
United Kingdom**

10

Distribution

Worldwide
APA Publications GmbH & Co. Verlag KG
(Singapore branch)
7030 Ang Mo Kio Ave 5
08-65 Northstar @ AMK, Singapore 569880
Email: apasin@singnet.com.sg

UK and Ireland
Dorling Kindersley Ltd
(a Penguin Company)
80 Strand, London, WC2R 0RL, UK
Email: sales@uk.dk.com

US
Ingram Publisher Services
One Ingram Blvd, PO Box 3006
La Vergne, TN 37086-1986
Email: customer.service@ingrampublisher
services.com

Australia
Universal Publishers
PO Box 307
St. Leonards NSW 1590
Email: sales@universalpublishers.com.au

Life

People

address *n*
Can you give me your ***address*** *please?*

la dirección
[la dee•rehk•theeyohn] *n*
¿Me da su ***dirección****, por favor?*

to be *v*
I ***am*** *hungry.*

tener [teh•nehr] *v*
Tengo *hambre.*

to be … years old *n*
The little one ***is*** *eight* ***years' old****.*

tener … años
[teh•nehr ah•nyohs] *locution*
La pequeña ***tiene*** *ocho* ***años****.*

beautiful *(f) adj*
The girl is ***beautiful****.*

guapa [gwah•pah] *adj*
Es una chica ***guapa****.*

better *adj*
My mobile is ***better*** *than Juan's.*

mejor (pl mejores)
[meh•khohr] *adj*
Mi móvil es ***mejor*** *que el de Juan.*

the best
*It is the **best** wine I have
ever drunk.*

el/la mejor (pl los/las mejores)
[ehl/lah meh·khohr] *adj*
*Es **el mejor** vino que he bebido
hasta ahora.*

12

boy *n*
*The **boy** is really cute.*

el chico [el chee·koh] *n*
***El chico** es muy cariño.*

centimeter *n*
*Pedro has already grown five
centimetres this year.*

el centímetro
[ehl thehn·tee·meh·troh] *n*
*Pedro ha crecido ya cinco
centímetros este año.*

to dream of *v*
*I **dream of** going to live abroad.*

soñar con [soh·nyahr kohn] *v*
***Sueña con** irse a vivir al extranjero.*

girl *n abbr* **Miss**
*A **girl** came to see you.*

Miss Fernandez has not
arrived yet.
Miss, you've dropped something
from your bag!

la señorita
[lah seh·nyoh·ree·tah] *n abbr* **Srta**.
*Una **señorita** ha venido a verte.*
***La señorita** Fernández todavía no
ha llegado.*
*¡**Señorita**, se le ha caído algo del
bolso!*

good *adj*
*Ricardo is a **good** friend.*

bueno, -a [booeh·noh,nah] *adj*
*Ricardo es un **buen** amigo.*

handsome (m)
*You're looking **handsome** today!*

guapo [gwah·poh] *adj*
*¡Qué **guapo** estás hoy!*

happy *adj*
*Carlos is a **happy** person.*

alegre [ah·leh·greh] *adj*
*Carlos es una persona **alegre**.*

to hear n
*I can **hear** the neighbours.*
Do you like to listen to the radio?

oír [oh·eer] *v*
***Oigo** a los vecinos.*
*¿Quieres **oír** la radio?*

his/her *pron*
*Paul has received a letter from
his parents.*

sus [soos] *pron m/f pl*
*Paul ha recibido una carta de **sus**
padres.*

her *pron*
*Juan is talking to **her**.*

ella [eh·yah] *pron f (after prep)*
*Juan habla con **ella**.*

I *pron*
***I**'ve just arrived.*

yo [yoh] *pron m/f*
***Yo** acabo de llegar.*

identity card n
*Your **identity card** please.*

el carné (de identidad)
[ehl kahr·neh (dehee·dehn·tee
·dahd)] *n*
*Su **carné de identidad**, por favor.*

to like *v*	**gustar** [goos•tahr] *v*
I really **like** this coat.	Me **gusta** mucho este abrigo.
lady *n abbr* **Mrs.**	**la señora** [lah seh•nyoh•rah] *n*
	abbr **Sra.**
Who is this **lady**?	¿Quién es aquella **señora**?
Mrs. Diaz called me.	La **señora** Díaz me ha llamado.
to look at *v*	**mirar** [mee•rahr] *v*
Stop **looking** at me like that!	¡Deja de **mirarme** así!
madam *n abbr* **Mrs.**	**señora** [seh•nyoh•rah] *n abbr* **Sra.**
Please sign here **madam**.	**Señora**, firme aquí, por favor.
Would you like a coffee, **Mrs.** Torres?	¿Quiere que le sirva un café, **señora** Torres?
man *n*	**el hombre** [ehl ohm•breh] *n*
Who will be the first **man** to walk on Mars?	¿Quién será el primer **hombre** que pise Marte?
man/gentleman *n*	**el señor** [ehl seh•nyohr] *n*
A **man** told me.	Me lo ha dicho un **señor**.
me *pron*	**me** [meh] *pron m/f*
Nobody loves **me**.	Nadie **me** quiere.
Can you pass **me** the book?	¿**Me** das el libro?

mister n abbvr. **Mr.**
Mr. Robles is on holidays abroad.

el señor [ehl seh·nyohr] n abbr **Sr.**
El señor Robles está de viaje al extranjero.

my pron
My friend is still a young man.

My sister lives in the countryside.

mi (pl mis) [mee] pron m/f
Mi amigo es todavía un hombre joven.

Mi hermana vive en el campo.

our pron
Our son is studying in England.

I need **our** blanket.

nuestro, -a (pl nuestros, nuestras) [noo·ehs·troh, trah]pron
Nuestro hijo está estudiando en Inglaterra.
Necesito **nuestra** manta.

**to be pleased /
happy for someone** v
We are **pleased** about the news.

alegrarse [ah·leh·grahr·seh] v pr

Nos **alegramos** de la noticia.

scared n
The child is **scared** at night.

el miedo [ehl meeyeh·doh] n
El niño tiene **miedo** por las noches.

she pron
She's very nice.

ella [eh·yah] pron f sg
Ella es muy simpática.

short adj
Pepe is not **short**.

bajo, -a [bah·khoh,khah] adj
No, Pepe no es **bajo**.

sir/ mister n abbr **Mr.**
Can I help you **sir**?
Is someone looking after you
Mr. Gomez?

señor [seh•nyohr] n abbr **Sr.**
¿**Señor**, me puede ayudar?
¿Alguien le atiende, **señor** Gomez?

tall adj
Sofia is as **tall** as her sister.

alto, -a [ahl•toh,tah] adj
Sofía es tan **alta** como su hermana.

their pron
The children have received a
letter from **their** parents.
There are Paloma and Carmen
with **their** friends.

sus [soos] pron m/f pl
Los niños han recibido una carta de
sus padres.
Allí está Paloma y Carmen con **sus**
amigas.

time n
It's the first **time** I've seen
your sister.

la vez [lah behth] n
Es la primera **vez** que veo a tu
Hermana

ugly adj
Juan is not **ugly** at all.

feo, -a [feh•oh,ah] adj
Juan no es nada **feo**.

woman n
She is a young **woman**.

la mujer [lah moo•khehr] n
Es una **mujer** joven.

you pron
Do **you** remember me?

te [teh] pron m/f
¿**Te** acuerdas de mí?

you pron (polite form)
Hello, can I help **you**?

le [leh] pron m/f
Buenos días, ¿**le** puedo ayudar?

your pron (polite form)
Mister Garcia, **your** suitcases
have already arrived.
Mr and Mrs Garcia, **your**
suitcases have already arrived.

sus [soos] pron m/f pl
Señor García, **sus** maletas ya han
llegado.
Señores García, **sus** maletas ya han
llegado.

to visit v
*Did you go **to visit** your mother?*

visitar [bee·see·tahr] v
*¿Ya has **visitado** a tu madre?*

Family

to be n
Cristian is my brother.
*Pilar **is** very beautiful.*

ser [sehr] v
*Cristian **es** mi hermano.*
*Pilar **es** muy guapa*

to be afraid of

*He is **afraid** of the dark.*

tener miedo a [teh·nehr
meeyeh·doh ah] *locution*
*Tiene **miedo a** la oscuridad.*

bad adv
*I slept **badly**.*

mal [mahl] adv
*He dormido **mal**.*

to bother v
*Is the music **bothering** you,
Mr. Garcia?*

molestar [moh·lehs·tahr] v
*¿Le **molesta** la música, señor García?*

breastfeed n
*Anna is **breastfeeding** the baby.*

dar el pecho [dahr ehl pehchoh] n
*Ana **da el pecho** al bébé.*

brother n
*My **brother** is called Luis.*

el hermano [ehl ehr·mah·noh] n
*Mi **hermano** se llama Luis.*

brothers and sisters n

There are three of us.

los hermanos
[lohs ehr·mah·nohs] n
*Somos tres **hermanos**.*

child (boy) n
*This **child** is very beautiful.*

el niño [ehl nee·nyoh] n f
*Este **niño** es muy guapo.*

child (girl) n
*My brother has two **children**.*

la niña [lah nee·nyah] n f
*Mi hermano tiene dos **niñas**.*

daughter n
*Have you seen my **daughter**?*

la hija [lah ee•khah] n f
*¿Has visto a mi **hija**?*

family n
*How is your **family**?*

la familia [lah fah•mee•leeyah] n
*¿Cómo está tu **familia**?*

father n
*My **father** still works.*

el padre [ehl pah•dreh] n m
*Mi **padre** trabaja todavía.*

fiance / boyfriend n
*This is Thomas, my daughter's **fiance/boyfriend**.*

el novio [ehl noh•beeyoh] n m
*Mira, ese es Tomás, **el novio** de mi hija.*

fiancee / girlfriend n
*Is it your **girlfriend** or are you just good friends?*

la novia [lah noh•beeyah] n f
*¿Es tu **novia** o sois solamente buenos amigos?*

friend n

el amigo [ehl ah•mee•goh] n
la amiga [lah ah•mee•gah] n

*He is a good **friend** of Pilar's.*
*Is Luis your boyfriend or just a **friend**?*
*My mother has lots of **friends** (feminine plural).*

*Es un buen **amigo** de Pilar.*
*¿Luis es su amigo o solo un **amigo**?*

*Mi madre tiene muchas **amigas***

to get along with v

entenderse
[ehn•tehn•dehr•seh] v pr

*Andres does not **get along** well **with** his family.*

*Andrés no **se entiende** bien con su familia.*

girl n
*They have two children, a boy and a **girl**.*
*The **girl** who lives on the second floor is Peruvian.*

la chica [lah chee•kah] n f
*Tienen dos hijos, un chico y una **chica**.*
***La chica** que vive en el segundo piso es peruana.*

grandfather n
My **grandfather** is 83 years old.

el abuelo [ehl ah·booeh·loh] n m
Mi **abuelo** tiene 83 años.

grandmother n
My **grandmother** is on the beach.

la abuela [lah ah·booeh·lah] n f
Mi **abuela** está en la playa.

his/her pron
Marcos has received a letter
from **his** father.
There's Paloma with **her**
best friend.

su [soo] pron m/f
Marcos ha recibido una carta de **su**
padre.
Allí está Paloma con **su** mejor
amiga.

to hope v
I **hope** my husband will come.

esperar [ehs·peh·rahr] v
Espero que venga mi marido.

husband n
How is your **husband**, Beatriz?

el marido [ehl mah·ree·doh] n
¿Cómo está tu **marido**, Beatriz?

to invite v
I **invited** your mother.

invitar [een·bee·thar] v
He **invitado** a tu madre.

like adv
This boy is **like** his father.

como [koh·moh] adv
Este chico es **como** su padre.

to love v
I **love** Marta very much.

querer [keh·rehr] v
Quiero mucho a Marta.

married adj
He is **married** to my sister.

casado, -a [kah·sah·doh] adj
Está **casado** con mi hermana.

mother n
My **mother** lives in the centre
of town.

la madre [lah mah·dreh] n f
Mi **madre** vive en el centro.

name n
I didn't hear his **name**.

el nombre [ehl nohm·breh] n
No he entendido su **nombre**.

Pedro is my first **name**, Sanchez is my surname.	Pedro es mi **nombre**, Sanchez mi apellido.
parents n My **parents** are very tolerant.	**los padres** [lohs pah·drehs] n Mis **padres** son muy tolerantes.
to recognise v Yes, I **recognise** him.	**darse cuenta de** [dahr·seh koo·ehn·tah deh] v pr Sí, **me he dado cuenta de** ello.
sister n My **sister** is sick.	**la hermana** [lah ehr·mah·nah] n Mi **hermana** está enferma.
small adj The children are still **small**.	**pequeño, -a** [peh·keh·nyoh, nyah] adj Los niños son todavía **pequeños**.
son n My **son** is studying in Paris.	**el hijo** [ehl ee·khoh] n Mi **hijo** está estudiando en París.
sons and daughters/children n I have three **children**.	**los hijos** [lohs ee·khohs] n Tengo three **hijos**.
surname n Carmen has a really long **surname**.	**el apellido** [ehl ah·peh·yee·doh] n Carmen tiene un **apellido** muy largo.

Fact

Spaniards and Latinos always have two surnames: the first is their father's, which is then followed by their mother's surname. For example, if **Juan Sánchez Molero** and **Carmen López Vela** were to have a child named Ana, their daughter's full name would be **Ana Sánchez López**, or **Ana López Sánchez**, which has also become acceptable of late.

their *pron*
The children have received a
letter from **their** father.
There are Paloma and Carmen
with **their** best friend.

su [soo] *pron m/f*
Los niños han recibido una carta de
su padre.
Allí está Paloma y Carmen con **su**
mejor amiga.

---

them *pron*
The children are in the garden.
Shall I bring **them** a glass of milk?

les [lehs] *pron m/f pl*
Los niños están en el jardín.
¿**Les** llevo un vaso de leche?

---

they *pron*
I saw Juana and Maria,
but **they** didn't notice.

ellas [eh·yahs] *pron f pl*
He visto a Juana y María, pero **ellas**
no se han dado cuenta.

---

they *pron*
I saw Juan and Pepe,
but **they** didn't notice.

ellos [eh·yohs] *pron m pl*
He visto a Juan y Pepe, pero **ellos** no
se han dado cuenta.

---

you *pron sg*
You're Jacinto, aren't **you**?

tú [too] *pron m/f*
Tú eres Jacinto, ¿no?

---

you *pron sg (polite form)*

I'm going to come with **you**.

usted [oos·tehd] *pron m/f*
(after prep)
Voy a ir con **usted**.

---

you *pron pl (polite form)*

Are **you** Spanish?

ustedes
[oos·teh·dehs] *pron m/f pl*
¿Son **ustedes** españolas?

---

young *adv*
Jose is **younger** than you.

joven [khoh·behn] *adv*
José es más **joven** que yo.

---

well / good *adv*
I'm very **well**.
You speak **good** Spanish.

bien [beeyehn] *adv*
Estoy muy **bien**.
Hablas **bien** español.

wife *n*
My **wife** is from Salamanca.

la mujer [lah moo·khehr] *n*
Mi **mujer** es de Salamanca.

worse *adv*
This wine is **worse** than the
other one.

peor (pl peores) [peh·ohr] *adj*
Este vino es **peor** que el otro.

the worst *adj*

It is the **worst** wine I have
ever bought.

el/la peor (pl los/las peores)
[ehl/lah peh·ohr] *adj*
Es **el peor** vino que he comprado
hasta ahora.

worse *adv*
My eyesight is **worse** than yours.

peor [peh·ohr] *adv*
Veo **peor** que tú.

your *pron sg*
Today I met **your** brother.

tu (pl tus) [too] *pron m/f*
Hoy he conocido a **tu** hermano.

your *pron pl*

Your son is already working,
isnt' he?

**vuestro, -a (pl vuestros,
vuestras)** [boo·ehs·troh, trah] *pron*
¿**Vuestro** hijo ya trabaja, ¿no?

your *pron (polite form)*
Mister Garcia, **your** car is
already fixed.
Mr and Mrs Garcia, **your** car
is already fixed.

su [soo] *pron m/f*
Señor García, **su** coche ya está
arreglado.
Señores García, **su** coche ya está
arreglado.

Countries & Languages

abroad n	**el extranjero** [ehl ex·trahn·kheh·roh] n
Many students travel **abroad**.	Muchos estudiantes viajan al **extranjero**.

- -

Africa n	**África** [ah·free·kah] n f
African adj	**africano, -a** [ah·free·kah·noh, nah] adj
	el africano [ehl ah·free·kah·noh] n
	la africana [lah ah·free·kah·nah] n

- -

to be v	**ser** [sehr] v
Are you from here?	¿**Es** usted de aquí?

Fact

Ser and **estar** are two Spanish verbs that can both be translated as 'to be' in English, but have quite distinct meanings in Spanish. **Ser** is used for names, origins, nationalities, professions, certain character traits and when giving the time. **Estar**, however, is used to describe transitional states or the geographical location of things and people, and for places.

Argentina n	**Argentina** [ahr·khehn·tee·nah] n f
Argentinian adj	**argentino, -a** [ahr·khehn·tee·noh,nah] adj
	el argentino [ehl ahr·khehn·tee·noh] n

la argentina
[lah ahr•khehn•tee•nah] *n*

Asia *n*	**Asia** [ah•seeyah] *n f*
Asian *adj*	**asiático, -a**
	[ah•seeyah•tee•koh,kah] *adj*
	el asiático [ehl ah•seeyah•tee•koh] *n*
	la asiática [lah ah•seeyah•tee•kah] *n*

Austria *n*	**Austria** [aws•treeyah] *n f*
Austrian *adj*	**austríaco, -a**
	[ah•oos•treeyah•koh, kah] *adj*
	el austríaco [ehl aws•treeyah•koh] *n*
	la austríaca [lah aws•treeyah•kah] *n*

Belgium *n*	**Bélgica** [behl•khee•kah] *n f*
Belgian	**belga** [behl•gah] *adj*
	el/la belga [ehl/lah behl•gah] *n*

Bolivia *n*	**Bolivia** [boh•lee•beeyah] *n f*
Bolivian *adj*	**boliviano, -a**
	[boh•lee•beeyah•noh, nah] *adj*
	el boliviano
	[ehl boh•lee•beeyah•noh] *n*
	la boliviana
	[lah boh•lee•beeyah•nah] *n*

Canada *n*	**(el) Canadá** [kah•nah•dah] *n m*
Canadian *adj*	**canadiense**
	[kah•nah•deeyehn•seh] *adj*
	el/la canadiense
	[ehl/lah kah•nah•deeyehn•seh] *n*

Central America *n*	**América Central** [ah•meh•ree•kah thehn•trahl] *n f* **Centroamérica** [then•troh•ah•meh•ree•kah]
Central American *adj*	**centroamericano, -a** [then•troh•ah•meh•ree•kah•noh, nah] *adj* **el centroamericano** [ehl then•troh•ah•meh•ree•kah•noh] *n* **la centroamericana** [lah then•troh•ah•meh•ree•kah•nah] *n*

Chile *n*	**Chile** [chee•leh] *n m*
Chilean *adj*	**chileno, -a** [chee•leh•noh,nah] *adj* **el chileno** [ehl chee•leh•noh] *n* **la chilena** [lah chee•leh•nah] *n*

Colombia *n*	**Colombia** [koh•lohm•beeyah] *n f*
Columbian *adj*	**colombiano, -a** [koh•lohm•beeyah•noh, nah] *adj* **el colombiano** [ehl koh•lohm•beeyah•noh] *n* **la colombiana** [lah koh•lohm•beeyah•nah] *n*

Costa Rica	**Costa Rica** [kohs•tah ree•kah] *n f*
Costa Rican *adj*	**costarricense** [kohs•tah•rree•thehn•seh] *adj* **costarriqueño, -a** [kohs•tah•rree•keh•nyoh,nyah] **el costarricense** [ehl kohs•tah•rree•thehn•seh] *n*

el costarriqueño
[ehl kohs•tah•rree•keh•nyoh]
la costarricense
[lah kohs•tah•rree•thehn•seh] *n*
la costarriqueña
[lah kohs•tah•rree•keh•nyah]

Cuba *n*   **Cuba** [koo•bah] *n f*
Cuban *adj*   **cubano, -a** [koo•bah•noh,nah] *adj*
       el cubano [ehl koo•bah•noh] *n*
       la cubana [lah koo•bah•nah] *n*

Dominican Republic *n* **República Dominicana**
       [reh•poo•blee•kah
       doh•mee•nee•kah•nah] *n f*
Dominican *adj*   **dominicano, -a**
       [doh•mee•nee•kah•noh,nah] *adj*
       el dominicano
       [ehl doh•mee•nee•kah•noh] *n*
       la dominicana
       [lah doh•mee•nee•kah•nah] *n*

Ecuador *n*   **Ecuador** [eh•koo•ah•dohr] *n m*
Ecuadorian *adj* **ecuatoriano, -a**
       [eh•koo•ah•toh•reeah•noh,nah] *adj*
       el ecuatoriano
       [ehl eh•koo•ah•toh•reeah•noh] *n*
       la ecuatoriana
       [lah eh•koo•ah•toh•reeah•nah] *n*

El Salvador *n*   **El Salvador** [ehl sahl•bah•dohr] *n m*
Salvadorean adj **salvadoreño, -a**
       [sahl•bah•doh•reh•nyoh,nyah] *adj*

el salvadoreño
[ehl sahl·bah·doh·reh·nyoh] *n*
la salvadoreña
[lah sahl·bah·doh·reh·nyah] *n*

England *n* — **Inglaterra** [een·glah·teh·rrah] *n f*
English *adj* — **inglés, inglesa (pl ingleses)**
[een·glehs, een·gleh·sah] *adj*
el inglés [ehl een·glehs] *n*
la inglesa [lah een·gleh·sah] *n*
(pl los ingleses)

English *n* — **inglés** [ehl een·glehs] *n m*

*My father speaks perfect **English**.* — *Mi padre habla **inglés** perfectamente.*

Europe *n* — **Europa** [ew·roh·pah] *n f*
European *adj* — **europeo, -a**
[ew·roh·peh·oh,peh·ah] *adj*
el europeo [ehl ew·roh·peh·oh] *n*
la europea [lah ew·roh·peh·ah] *n*

foreigner *n* — **el extranjero**
[ehl ex·trahn·kheh·roh] *m n*
la extranjera
[lah ex·trahn·kheh·rah] *f n*

*A lot of **foreigners** live in this region.* — *En esta región viven muchos **extranjeros**.*
*I'm a **foreigner**.* — *Yo soy **extranjera**.*

foreign *adj* — **extranjero, -a**
[ex·trahn·kheh·roh,rah] *adj*

*I prefer **foreign** wines.* — *Me gustan más los vinos **extranjeros**.*

France *n*
French *adj*

Francia [frahn•theeah] *n f*
francés, francesa (pl franceses)
[frahn•thehs,theh•sah] *adj*
el francés [ehl frahn•thehs] *n*
la francesa [lah frahn•theh•sah] *n*
*(pl **los franceses**)*

*Does anyone here speak **French**?*   *¿Hay alguien aquí que hable **francés**?*

from *prep*
*George is **from** Malaga.*

de [deh] *prep*
*Jorge es **de** Málaga.*

Germany *n*
***Germany** exports lots of cars.*
This year we are going on
*holidays to **Germany**.*
German *adj*

*My friend Ulrike is **German**.*
*My parents are **German**.*
German *n*

*Lots of **Germans** come*
in summer.
*Do you speak **German**?*

Alemania [ah•leh•mah•neeyah] *n f*
***Alemania** exporta muchos coches.*
Este año vamos de vacaciones a
***Alemania**.*
alemán, alemana (pl alemanes)
[ah•leh•mahn, ah•leh•mah•nah] *adj*
*Mi amiga Ulrike es **alemana**.*
*Mis padres son **alemanes**.*
el alemán [ehl ah•leh•mahn] *n*
la alemana [lah ah•leh•mah•nah] *n*
(pl los alemanes)
Aquí en verano vienen muchos here
***alemanes**.*
*¿Habla usted **alemán**?*

Great Britain *n*

British *adj*

Gran Bretaña
[grahn breh•tah•nyah] *n f*
británico, -a
[bree•tah•nee•koh,kah] *adj*
el británico
[ehl bree•tah•nee•koh] *n*

	la británica [lah bree•tah•nee•kah] *n*
Guatemala *n* **Guatemalan**	**Guatemala** [gwah•teh•mah•lah] *n f* **guatemalteco, -a** [gwah•teh•mahl•teh•koh,kah] *adj* **el guatemalteco** [ehl gwah•teh•mahl•teh•koh] *n* **la guatemalteca** [lah gwah•teh•mahl•teh•kah] *n*
he *pron* **He** speaks better Spanish than she does.	**él** [ehl] *pron m sg* **Él** habla mejor español que ella.
Honduras *n* **Honduran** *adj*	**Honduras** [ohn•doo•rahs] *n m* **hondureño, -a** [ohn•doo•reh•nyoh,nyah] *adj* **el hondureño** [ehl ohn•doo•reh•nyoh] *n* **la hondureña** [lah ohn•doo•reh•nyah] *n*
international *adj* It's an **international** problem.	**internacional (pl internacionales)** [een•tehr•nah•theeyoh•nahl] *adj* Es un problema **internacional**.
Italy *n* **Italian** *adj*	**Italia** [ee•tah•leeah] *n f* **italiano, -a** [ee•tah•leeah•noh,nah] *adj* **el italiano** [ehl ee•tah•leeah•noh] *n* **la italiana** [lah ee•tah•leeah•nah] *n*

Italian n
*My sister is studying **Italian**.*

el italiano [ehl ee•tah•leeah•noh] n
*Mi hija está estudiando **italiano**.*

Language n
*Carmen speaks three **languages**.*

el idioma [ehl ee•deeyoh•mah] n
*Carmen habla tres **idiomas**.*

Latin American n

Latinoamérica
[lah•tee•noh•ah•meh•ree•kah] n f
América Latina

Latin American n

latinoamericano, -a [lah•tee•noh
•ah•meh•ree•kah•noh,nah] adj
el latinoamericano [ehl
lah•tee•noh•ah•meh•ree•kah•noh] n
la latinoamericana [lah
lah•tee•noh•ah•meh•ree•kah•nah] n

Luxemburg n

Luxemburgo
[loo•xehm•boor•goh] n m

Luxemburger adj

**luxemburgués, luxemburguesa
(pl luxemburgueses)**
[loo•xehm•boor•gehs, geh•sah] adj
el luxemburgués
[ehl loo•xehm•boor•gehs] n
la luxemburguesa
[lah loo•xehm•boor•geh•sah] n
(pl los luxemburgueses)

Mexico n

México [meh•xee•koh] n m
also **Méjico** [meh•khee•koh]

Mexican adj

mexicano, -a
[meh•xee•kah•noh,nah] adj
mejicano, -a
[meh•khee•kah•noh,nah]

el mexicano [el mexiˈkano] *n*
el mejicano
[ehl meh•xee•kah•noh]
la mexicana [la mexiˈkana] *n*
la mejicana
[lah meh•xee•kah•nah]

---

national *adj*

Football is a **national** passion.

nacional (pl nacionales)
[nah•theeyoh•nahl] *adj*
El fútbol es una pasión **nacional**.

---

nationality *n*

What **nationality** are you,
Mrs. Vivar?
I have dual **nationality**.

la nacionalidad
[lah nah•theeyoh•nah•lee•dahd] *n*
¿Qué **nacionalidad** tiene usted,
señora Vivar?
Tengo doble **nacionalidad**.

Nicaragua *n*
Nicaraguan

Nicaragua [nee•kah•rah•gwah] *n*
nicaragüense
[nee•kah•rah•gwehn•seh] *adj*
nicaragüeño, -a
[nee•kah•rah•gweh•nyoh,nyah]
el nicaragüense
[ehl nee•kah•rah•gwehn•seh] *n*
el nicaragüeño
[ehl nee•kah•rah•gweh•nyoh]
la nicaragüense
[lah nee•kah•rah•gwehn•seh] *n*
el nicaragüeño,
la nicaragüeña
[ehl nee•kah•rah•gweh•nyoh, lah
nee•kah•rah•gweh•nyah]

North America *n*	**América del Norte** [ah•meh•ree•kah dehl nohr•teh] *n f* **Norteamérica** [nohr•teh•ah•meh•ree•kah]
North American *adj*	**norteamericano, -a** [nohrteh•ahmehree•kah•noh,nah] **el norteamericano** [ehl nohr•teh•ah•meh•ree•kah•noh] *n* **la norteamericana** [lah nohr•teh•ah•meh•ree•kah•nah] *n*
Panama **Panamanian** *adj*	**Panamá** [pah•nah•mah] *n m* **panameño, -a** [pah•nah•meh•nyoh,nyah] *adj* **el panameño** [ehl pah•nah•meh•nyoh] *n* **la panameña** [lah pah•nah•meh•nyah] *n*
Paraguay *n* **Paraguayan** *n*	**Paraguay** [pah•rah•gwaye] *n m* **paraguayo, -a** [pah•rah•gwah•yoh,yah] *adj* **el paraguayo** [ehl pah•rah•gwah•yoh] *n* **la paraguaya** [lah pah•rah•gwah•yah] *n*
Peru *n* **Peruvian** *adj*	**el Perú** [peh•roo] *n m* **peruano, -a** [peh•roo•ah•noh,nah] *adj* **el peruano** [ehl peh•roo•ah•noh] *n* **la peruana** [lah peh•roo•ah•nah] *n*

Portugal n	**Portugal** [pohr·too·gahl] n m
Portuguese n	**portugués, portuguesa** [pohr·too·gehs, pohr·too·geh·sah] adj
	el portugués [ehl pohr·too·gehs] n
	la portuguesa [lah pohr·too·geh·sah] n
	(pl los portugueses)
Portuguese n	**el portugués** [ehl pohr·too·gehs] n m
Do you speak **Portuguese**?	¿Tú hablas **portugués**?
Puerto Rico n	**Puerto Rico** [poo·ehrtoh reekoh] n
Puerto Rican adj	**puertoriqueño, -a** [poo·ehr·toh·ree·keh·nyoh,nyah] adj
	el puertoriqueño [ehl poo·ehr·toh·ree·keh·nyoh] n
	la puertoriqueña [lah poo·ehr·toh·ree·keh·nyah] n
since prep	**desde hace** [dehs·deh ah·theh] prep
We have been living here for a year.	Vivimos aquí **desde hace** un año.

Fact

Desde and **Desde hace** can both mean 'since'. **Desde** is used in relation to a starting point in time, i.e. since yesterday, with yesterday being the starting point. **Desde hace** refers to a duration in time. See **Desde** on page 115.

South America *n*	**América del Sur** [ah·meh·ree·kah dehl soor] *n f* **Sudamérica** [sood·ah·meh·ree·kah] **sudamericano, -a** [sood·ah·meh·ree·kah·noh,nah] *adj*
South American *adj*	**el sudamericano** [ehl sood·ah·meh·ree·kah·noh] *n* **la sudamericana** [lah sood·ah·meh·ree·kah·nah] *n*
Spain *n*	**España** [esh·pah·nyah] *n f*
Spanish *adj*	**español, española (pl españoles)** [esh·pah·nyohl,nyoh·lah] *adj* **el español** [ehl esh·pah·nyohl] *n* **la española** [lah eshpahnyohlah] *(pl los españoles)*
*You speak good **Spanish**.*	*Usted habla bien **español**.*
Basque *n* *Do you speak the **Basque** language?*	**el vasco** [ehl bahs·koh] *n* *¿Habla usted **el vasco**?*
Catalan *n* *Do you speak **Catalan**?*	**el catalán** [ehl kah·tah·lahn] *n* *¿Habla usted **catalán**?*

Fact

In Spain, when referring to the Spanish language you would normally use the term **el castellano**, Castilian.

Fact

Basque is the only non-Romance language in Spain and to this day its origin is still unclear. Basque is spoken in the North West, in the Basque Country, in a part of Navarre and in the French Basque Country. It is one of the four regional languages of Spain and is also called **el euskera**.

Galician *n*	**el gallego** [ehl gah·yeh·goh] *n*
Do you speak **Galician**?	¿Habla usted **gallego**?
Switzerland *n*	**Suiza** [soo·ee·thah] *n f*
Swiss *adj*	**suizo, -a** [soo·ee·thoh,thah] *adj*
	el suizo [ehl soo·ee·thoh] *n*
	la suiza [lah soo·ee·thah] *n*

Fact

Galician is spoken in the North East of Spain and is the second official administrative language in the Galicia along with Spanish. It is very close to Portuguese.

United States *n*	**(los) Estados Unidos** [(lohs) ehs·tah·dohs oo·nee·dohs] *n pl m*
American *adj*	**estadounidense** [ehs·tah·dohoo·nee·dehn·seh] *adj*
	el/la estadounidense [ehl/lah ehs·tah·dohoo·nee·dehn·seh] *n*

Uruguay *n*	**Uruguay** [oo•roo•gwaye] *n m*
Uruguayan *adj*	**uruguayo, -a** [oo•roo•gwah•yoh, yah] *adj*
	el uruguayo [ehl oo•roo•gwah•yoh] *n*
	la uruguaya [lah oo•roo•gwah•yah] *n*
Venezuela *n*	**Venezuela** [beh•neh•thooeh•lah] *n f*
Venezuelan *adj*	**venezolano, -a** [beh•neh•thoh•lah•noh,nah] *adj*
	el venezolano [ehl beh•neh•thoh•lah•noh] *n*
	la venezolana [lah beh•neh•thoh•lah•nah] *n*
what *pron*	**qué** [keh] *pron*
What *good Spanish you have!*	*¡**Qué** bien habla usted español!*
What *a lovely house!*	*¡**Qué** casa tan bonita!*
you *pron sg (polite form)*	**usted** [oos•tehd] *pron m/f sg*
*Are **you** Spanish?*	*¿Es **usted** española?*

Nature & Animals

animal *n*	**el animal (pl los animales)** [ehl ah•nee•mahl] *n*
*I like **animals** a lot.*	*Me gustan mucho los **animales**.*

bird n	**el pájaro** [ehl pah·kha·roh] n
Can't you hear the **birds**?	¿No oyes los **pájaros**?
cat n	**la gata** [lah gah·tah] n
My **cat** is called Aphrodite.	Mi **gata** se llama Afrodita.
tomcat n	**el gato** [ehl gah·toh] n
What a lovely **tomcat**!	¡Qué **gato** tan bonito!
chicken n	**la gallina** [lah gah·yee·nah] n
Chickens lay eggs.	Las **gallinas** ponen huevos.
cockerel n	**el gallo** [ehl gah·yoh] n
The **cockerel** sings.	El **gallo** canta.
coast n	**la costa** [lah kohs·tah] n
Do you know the **coast** already?	¿Ya conocéis **la costa**?
country n	**el país (pl los paises)** [ehl pah·ees] n
Would you like to know this **country**?	¿Quieres conocer este **país**?
countryside n	**el campo** [ehl kahm·poh] n
Do you like living in the **countryside**?	¿Le gusta vivir en **el campo**?
cow n	**la vaca** [lah bah·kah] n
I drink a lot of **cow's** milk.	Bebo mucha leche de **vaca**.
dog n	**el perro** [ehl peh·rroh] n
The **dog** is in the garden.	**El perro** está en el jardín.
fish n	**el pez (pl los peces)** [ehl pehth] n
There are lots of **fish** in this river.	Hay muchos **peces** en este río.

flower n
*I have **flowers** of every colour in my garden.*

la flor (pl las flores) [lah flohr]n
*En mi jardín hay **flores** de todos los colores.*

fly n
*There are lots of **flies** in the country house.*

la mosca [lah mohs·kah] n
*En la casa de campo hay muchas **moscas**.*

forest n
*The house is close to the **forest**.*

el bosque [ehl bohs·keh] n
*La casa está cerca del **bosque**.*

goat n
*My mother likes **goat's** milk very much.*

la cabra [lah kah·brah] n
*A mi madre le gusta mucho el queso de **cabra**.*

grass n
*Cows eat **grass**.*

la hierba [lah eeyehr·bah] n
*Las vacas comen **hierba**.*

horse n
*Argentine **horses** are famous famosos worldwide.*

el caballo [ehl kah·bah·yoh] n
*Los **caballos** argentinos son en todo el mundo.*

lake n
*There's a lovely **lake** five kilometers from here.*

el lago [ehl lah·goh] n
*A cinco kilómetros de aquí hay un **lago** muy bonito.*

landscape n
*The **landscape** is very impressive.*

el paisaje [ehl pahee·sah·kheh] n
*Los **paisajes** son impresionantes.*

leaf n
*Many trees lose their **leaves** in autumn.*

la hoja [lah oh·khah] n
*En otoño muchos árboles pierden las **hojas**.*

mountain n

la montaña [lah mohn·tah·nyah] n

*I prefer the **mountains** to the sea.* | *Me gusta más la **montaña** que el mar.*

mouse n | **el ratón (pl los ratones)** [ehl ra·tohn] n

*This **mouse** is white.* | *Este **ratón** es blanco.*

pig n | **el cerdo** [ehl thehr·doh] n
*On the farm we saw cows and **pigs**.* | *En la granja vimos vacas y cerdos.*

palm tree n | **la palmera** [lah pahl·meh·rah] n
*These **palm trees** are very high.* | *Estas **palmeras** son muy altas.*

place n | **el sitio** [ehl see·teeyoh] n
*This is the quietest **place** in town.* | *Es el **sitio** más tranquilo de la ciudad.*

plant n | **la planta** [lah plahn·tah] n
*The **plant** needs more water.* | *La **planta** necesita más agua.*

rabbit n | **el conejo** [ehl koh·neh·khoh] n
*Carmen has two **rabbits** in the garden.* | *Carmen tiene dos **conejos** en el jardín.*

region n | **la región (pl las regiones)** [lah reh·kheeyohn] n
*There is a lot of industry in this **region**.* | *En esta **región** hay muchas industrias.*

river n | **el río** [ehl ree·oh] n
*What's this **river** called?* | *¿Cómo se llama este **río**?*

rose n | **la rosa** [lah roh·sah] n
*A **rose** for you.* | *Una **rosa** roja para usted.*

sea n	el mar [ehl mahr] n
I like going to the **sea**.	Me gusta ir al **mar**.
spider n	la araña [lah ah•rah•nyah] n
I'm scared of **spiders**.	Tengo miedo a las **arañas**.
tree n	el árbol (pl los árboles) [ehl ahr•bohl] n
We have four big **trees** in our garden.	Tenemos cuatro grandes **árboles** en nuestro jardín.
village n	el pueblo [ehl pweh•bloh] n
I really like coastal **villages**.	Me gustan mucho los **pueblos** de la costa.
world n	el mundo [ehl moon•doh] n
Clara travels a lot, she knows the whole **world**.	Clara viaja mucho, conoce **el mundo** entero.

Describing Things

a art	un, una [uhN, ewnah] an art
That's **a** very nice car.	Es **un** coche muy bonito.
bad adj	malo, -a [mah•loh,lah] adj
How **bad** is this book!	¡Qué **malo** es este libro!
I have had a **bad** day.	He tenido un **mal** día.
This child is really naughty.	Este niño es realmente **malo**.
big adj	grande [grahn•deh] adj
The house is not very **big**.	La casa no es muy **grande**.
blue adj	azul (pl azules) [ah•thool] adj
I like the **blue** flowers.	Me gustan las flores **azules**.

Fact

Malo has two comparative forms and two superlative forms: **peor** (comparative)/**el peor** (superlative) and **más malo** (comparative)/ **el más malo** (superlative). Whereas **peor** as a superlative is placed before a noun, **más malo** on the other hand is placed after the noun: **el peor vino — el vino más malo.**

black *adj*
*The table I bought is **black**.*

negro, -a [neh·groh] *adj*
*La mesa que he comprado es **negra**.*

but *conj*
*She's not my sister **but** my daughter.*

sino [see·noh] *conj*
*No es mi hermana **sino** mi hija.*

clean *adj*
*The hotel is simple but **clean**.*

limpio, -a [leem·peeoh,peeah] *adj*
*El hotel es sencillo pero **limpio**.*

color *n*

*What **colour** table do you want Mrs Tesedo?*

el color (pl los colores) [ehl koh·lohr] *n*

*¿De qué **color** quiere la mesa, señora Tesedo?*

fast *adj*
*I have a very **fast** car.*

rápido, -a [rah·pee·doh,dah] *adj*
*Tengo un coche muy **rápido**.*

green *adj*
*My car is **green**.*

verde [behr·deh] *adj*
*Mi coche es **verde**.*

grey *adj*
*I want to buy a **grey** coat.*

gris (pl grises) [grees] *adj*
*Quiero comprarme un abrigo **gris**.*

large *adj*
*This sweater is a little **large**.*

largo, -a [lahr·goh,gah] *adj*
*Este jersey es un poco **largo**.*

new *adj*
Joe has a **new** car.

nuevo, -a [nooeh·boh,bah] *adj*
Joe tiene un coche **nuevo**.

old *adj*
My grandparents are very **old**.

viejo, -a [beeyeh·khoh,khah] *adj*
Mis abuelos son muy **viejos**.

poor *adj*
It's a **poor** country.

pobre [poh·breh] *adj*
Es un país **pobre**.

red *adj*
I like this **red** bag.

rojo, -a [roh·khoh,khah] *adj*
Me gusta este bolso **rojo**.

rich *adj*
I'm not **rich**.

rico, -a [ree·koh,kah] *adj*
No soy **rico**.

round *adj*

I prefer the **round** table.

redondo, -a
[reh·dohn·doh,dah] *adj*
La mesa **redonda** me gusta más.

shape *n*
What **shape** is the table, is it round or square?

la forma [lah fohr·mah] *n*
¿Qué **forma** tiene la mesa, es redonda o cuadrada?

short *adj*
This skirt is quite **short**.

corto, -a [kohr·toh,tah] *adj*
Esta falda es demasiado **corta**.

simple *adj*

It's a **simple** but good restaurant.

sencillo, -a
[sehn·thee·yoh,yah] *adj*
Es un restaurante **sencillo** pero bueno.

slow *adj*
This train is really **slow**.

lento, -a [lehn·toh,tah] *adj*
Este tren es muy **lento**.

square *adj*

cuadrado, -a
[kooah·drah·doh,dah] *adj*

I prefer the **square** table.	Me gusta más la mesa **cuadrada.**
the *art sing.*	**el** [ehl] *m art*
the chocolate	**el chocolate** [choh•koh•lah•teh] *n*
the *pron*	**la** [lah] *f art*
the salad	**la ensalada** [ehn•sah•lah•dah] *n*
the *art plural*	**los** [lohs] *m art*
the gardens	**los jardines** [khahr•dee•nehs] *n*
the *art plural*	**las** [lahs] *f art*
the omelettes	**las tortillas** [lah tohr•tee•yah] *n*
white *adj* Do you see this **white** house?	**blanco, -a** [blahn•koh,kah] *adj* ¿Ves esa casa **blanca?**
yellow *adj* Susan's new car is **yellow**.	**amarillo, -a** [ah•mah•ree•yoh,yah] *adj* El nuevo coche de Susan es **amarillo.**
young *adj* My parents are still **young**.	**joven (pl jovenes)** [khoh•beh•nehs] *adj* Mis padres todavía son **jóvenes.**

The Body

arm *n* I have a pain in my **arm**.	**el brazo** [ehl brah•thoh] *n* Me duele **el brazo.**
to comb *v* Why don't you **comb** your hair back?	**peinarse** [pehee•nahr•seh] *v pr* ¿Por qué no te **peinas** el pelo para atrás?

deodorant *n*

*Teresa uses another **deodorant**.*

el desodorante
[ehl deh·soh·doh·rahn·teh] *n*
*Teresa usa otro **desodorante**.*

eye *n*
*You have lovely **eyes**.*

el ojo [ehl oh·khoh] *n*
*Tienes unos **ojos** muy bonitos.*

facecloth *n*

*Do you have a **facecloth**?*

la manopla de baño
[lah mah·noh·plah deh bah·nyoh] *n*
*¿Tienes una **manopla de baño**?*

foot *n*
*I have a pain in my **feet**.*

el pie [ehl pee·eh] *n*
*Me duelen los **pies**.*

hair *n*
*My sister has really long **hair**.*

el pelo [ehl peh·loh] *n*
*Mi hermana tiene **el pelo** muy largo.*

hairbrush *n*
*I forgot my **hairbrush**.*

el cepillo [ehl theh·pee·yoh] *n*
*He olvidado **el cepillo** del pelo.*

hand *n*
*Give me your **hand** to cross the street.*

la mano [lah mah·noh] *n*
*Dame **la mano** para cruzar la calle.*

head *n*
*15 euros a **head***

la cabeza [lah kah·beh·thah] *n*
*15 euros por **cabeza***

finger *n*
*He wore a ring on his **finger**.*

el dedo [ehl deh·doh] *n*
*Llevaba un anillo en su **dedo**.*

knee *n*
*I'm going to have an operation on my **knee**.*

la rodilla [lah roh·dee·yah] *n*
*Me voy a operar de **la rodilla**.*

leg *n*
Elisa has long legs.

la pierna [lah pee·ehr·nah] *n*
*Elisa tiene **las piernas** largas.*

mouth n	**la boca** [lah boh·kah] n
*Open your **mouth**, please.*	*Abra **la boca**, por favor.*
nose n	**la nariz** [lah nah·reeth] n
*I want a **nose** job.*	*Me quiero operar **la nariz**.*
soap n	**el jabón** [ehl khah·bohn] n
*This **soap** smells really good.*	*Este **jabón** huele muy bien.*
shampoo n	**el champú** [ehl chahm·poo] n
*I forgot the **shampoo**.*	*Ha olvidado **el champú**.*
shoulder n	**la espalda** [lah ehs·pahl·dah] n
*I always have a pain in my **shoulder**.*	*Siempre me duele **la espalda**.*
shoulders n	**el hombro** [ehl ohm·broh] n
*He carried his son on his **shoulders**.*	*Llevaba a su hijo sobre **los hombros**.*
to shower v	**ducharse** [doo·chahr·seh] v pr
*Do you want a **shower**?*	*¿Quieres **ducharte**?*
shower gel n	**el gel de ducha** [ehl khehl deh doo·chah] n
*I bought some **shower gel**.*	*He comprado un gel de d**ucha**.*
skin n	**la piel** [lah pee·ehl] n
*Saltwater is good for the **skin**.*	*El agua de mar es buena para **la piel**.*
tissue n	**el pañuelo** [ehl pah·nyooeh·loh] n
*I always carry **tissues** on me.*	*Siempre llevo **pañuelos** de papel.*
toe n	**el dedo del pie** [ehl deh·doh dehl pee·eh] n

*I used to know a guy with six **toes** once upon a time.*	*Una vez conocí a un chico con seis **dedos del pie**.*
toilet roll n	**el papel higiénico** [ehl pah·pehl ee·gee·eh·nee·koh] n
*We need to buy **toilet roll**.*	*Tenemos que comprar **papel higiénico**.*
toothpaste n	**la pasta de dientes** [lah pahs·tah deh dee·ehn·tehs] n
*I need a tube of **toothpaste**.*	*Necesito un tubo de **pasta de dientes**.*
tooth n	**el diente** [ehl dee·ehn·teh] n
*I have lost a **tooth**.*	*Se me ha caído un **diente**.*
toothbrush n	**el cepillo de dientes** [ehl theh·pee·yoh deh dee·ehn·tehs] n
*Don't forget to pack your **toothbrush**.*	*¡No te olvides de meter en la maleta tu **cepillo de dientes**!*
towel n	**la toalla** [lah toh·ah·yah] n
*There are clean **towels** here.*	*Allí hay **toallas** limpias.*
to wash v	**lavarse** [lah·bahr·seh] v pr
*This child doesn't like to be **washed**.*	*A este niño no le gusta **lavarse**.*

Health & Emergencies

accident n	**el accidente** [ehl ak·theedehnteh]
*My parents have had a car **accident**.*	*Mis padres han tenido un **accidente** de coche.*

to be *v*
I'm already better.

estar [ehs·tahr] *v*
Ya **estoy** mejor.

---

blood *n*
The injured has lost a lot of **blood**.

la sangre [lah sahn·greh] *n*
El herido ha perdido mucha **sangre**.

---

cigarette *n*

You have forgotten the **cigarettes**.

el cigarrillo
[ehl thee·gah·rree·yoh] *n*
Habéis olvidado los **cigarillos**.

---

to be cold
Close the door, I'm **cold**.

tener frío [teh·nehr free·oh] *locution*
Cierra la puerta, **tengo frío**.

---

dentist *n*

I need to go to the **dentist**.

el/la dentista
[ehl/lah dehn·tees·tah] *n*
Tengo que ir al **dentista**.

---

doctor *n*
doctor *(f)* *n*
The **doctor** still hasn't arrived.

el doctor [ehl dohk·tohr] *n*
la doctora [lah dohk·toh·rah] *n*
El **doctor** todavía no ha llegado.

---

doctor *n*

I called the **doctor**.
I thought the **doctor** had
already arrived.

el médico [ehl meh·dee·koh] *n*
la médico [lah meh·dee·koh] *n*
(female doctor)
He llamado al **médico**.
Creo que **la médico** ya ha llegado.

---

to feel *v*
I don't **feel** well today.

sentirse [sehn·teer·seh] *v pr*
No me **siento** bien hoy.

---

to feel better *v*
The patient is **feeling better**.

mejor [meh·khohr] *adv*
El enfermo está **mejor**.

to have a cold v	resfriado, -a
	[rrehs·freeah·doh,dah] adj
I don't feel well, **I have a cold**.	No me siento bien, estoy **resfriada**.

headache n	**el dolor de cabeza**
	[ehl doh·lohr de kah·beh·thah] n
Do you have a **headache**?	¿Tiene usted **dolor de cabeza**?

| health n | **la salud** [lah sah·lood] n |
| **Health** is important. | **La salud** es muy importante. |

| healthy adj | **sano, -a** [sah·noh,nah] adj |
| Eating fruit is very **healthy**. | Comer fruta es muy **sano**. |

| hospital n | **el hospital** [ehl ohs·pee·tahl] n |
| We need to take him to **hospital**. | Hay que llevarlo al **hospital**. |

to be hot	tener calor
	[teh·nehr kah·lohr] locution
I am very **hot**.	**Tengo** mucho **calor**.

illness n	**la enfermedad**
	[lah ehn·fehr·meh·dahd] n
Luckily I have never had a	Por suerte no he tenido nunca una
serious **illness**.	**enfermedad** grave.

Fact

Hacer calor and **tener calor** express different things. **Hacer calor** is used when referring to heat in a general context ('it is hot' when talking about the weather), whereas **tener calor** is used to express the sensation, i.e. when you feel hot.

moment *n*

*Wait a **moment**, please.*

el momento
[ehl moh•mehn•toh] *n*
*Espere un **momento**, por favor.*

nurse *n*

*I work as a **nurse** in a hospital.*

la enfermera
[lah ehn•fehr•meh•rah] *n*
*Trabajo de **enfermera** en el hospital.*

pain *n*

*I have **pain** here.*

el dolor (pl los dolores)
[ehl doh•lohr] *n*
*Tengo **dolores** aquí.*

to have a pain in *v*
*Where do you have **pain** Mr Vásquez?*

doler [doh•lehr] *v*
¿Dónde le duele, señor Vázquez?

sick *adj*

*Isabel is **sick**, she is in bed.*

enfermo, -a [ehn•fehr•moh,mah] *adj*
*Isabel está **enferma**, está en la cama.*

pharmacy *n*

*Do you know where the **pharmacy** is?*

la farmacia
[lah fahr•mah•thee•ah] *n*
*¿Sabe usted dónde está **la farmacia**?*

fever *n*
*I have a high **fever**.*

la fiebre [lah feeyeh•breh] *n*
*Tengo mucha **fiebre**.*

to smoke *v*
*You cannot **smoke** here.*

fumar [foo•mahr] *v*
*Usted no puede **fumar** aquí.*

medicine *n*

*I have to take the **medicine** before eating.*

la medicina
[lah meh•dee•thee•nah] *n*
*Tengo que tomar **la medicina** antes de la comida.*

Fact

If the article **el** follows the preposition **a**, **a + el** becomes **al**, for example: **vamos al hospital**.

stomach ache *n*	**el dolor de vientre** [ehl doh•lohr deh bee•ehn•treh] *n*
Carlos no longer has a **stomach ache**.	*Carlos ya no tiene* **dolor de vientre**.
the **The** *important thing is your health.*	**lo** [low] **Lo** *importante es la salud.*
tired *adj* *Paloma is* **tired**.	**cansado, -a** [kahn•sah•doh,dah] *adj* *Paloma está* **cansada**.
toothache *n* *I have a terrible* **toothache**.	**el dolor de muelas** [ehl doh•lohr deh moo•eh•lahs] *n* *Tengo un terrible* **dolor de muelas**.
waiting room *n* *The* **waiting room** *is very big.*	**la sala de estar** [lah sah•lah deh ehs•tahr] *n* **La sala de estar** *es muy grande.*

Day to Day

At Home

as... as *adv*

My room is **as** big **as** Elena's.

tan ... como
[tahn ... koh•moh] *adv*

Mi habitación es **tan** grande **como** la de Elena.

---

balcony *n*

The flat has two **balconies**.

el balcón (pl los balcones)
[ehl bahl•kohn] *n*
El piso tiene dos **balcones**.

---

bathroom *n*
I have no more rooms with a **bathroom**.

el baño [ehl bah•nyoh] *n*
No me quedan habitaciones con **baño**.

---

bed *n*
How many times do I have to tell you to make your **bed**!

la cama [lah kah•mah] *n*
¡Cuantas veces tengo que repetirte que hagas **la cama**!

bedroom *n*	**el dormitorio**
	[ehl dohr•mee•toh•reeoh] *n*
*I'd like a more spacious **bedroom**.*	*Me gustaría tener un **dormitorio** más amplio.*
blanket *n*	**la manta** [lah mahn•tah] *n*
*It's cold, I need another **blanket**.*	*Hace frío, necesito otra **manta**.*
to break *v*	**estropearse**
	[ehs•troh•peh•ahr•seh] *v pr*
*The telephone is **broken**.*	*Se ha **estropeado** el teléfono.*
broken *adj*	**roto, -a** [roh•toh,tah] *adj*
*The glass is **broken**.*	*El vaso está **roto**.*
can *v*	**poder** [poh•dehr] *v*
cannot *v (can't)*	
*I **can't** get up.*	*No **puedo** levantarme.*
***Can** I come in?*	*¿**Puedo** entrar?*
card *n*	**la tarjeta** [lah tahr•kheh•tah] *n*
*I have lost the credit c**ard**.*	*He perdido **la tarjeta** de crédito.*
chair *n*	**la silla** [lah see•yah] *n*
*We're missing a c**hair**.*	*Falta una **silla**.*
to clean *v*	**limpiar** [leem•peeyahr] *v*
*I have just **cleaned** the glasses.*	*Acabo de **limpiar** los cristales.*
*Have you **cleaned** your room?*	*¿Ya habéis **limpiado** la habitación?*
comfortable *adj*	**cómodo, -a** [koh•moh•doh,dah] *adj*
*This bed is so **comfortable**!*	*¡Qué **cómoda** es esta cama!*
cooker *n*	**la cocina** [lah koh•thee•nah] *n*
*My **cooker** does not work.*	*Mi **cocina** no funciona.*

dirty *adj*	**sucio, -a** [soo•theeoh, theeah] *adj*
The swimming pool is **dirty**.	La piscina está **sucia**.
door *n*	**la puerta** [lah poo•ehr•tah] *n*
Close the **door** please.	Cierre **la puerta**, por favor.
to enter / come in *v*	**entrar** [ehn•trahr] *v*
Come in please!	¡**Entren**, por favor!
flat / floor *n*	**el piso** [ehl pee•soh] *n*
Carmen and Paco have bought a **flat**.	Carmen y Paco han comprado un **piso**.
Which **floor** do you live on?	¿En qué **piso** vivís?
fridge *n*	**la nevera** [lah neh•beh•rah] *n*
The beer is in the **fridge**.	La cerveza está en **la nevera**.
garden *n*	**el jardín** [ehl khahr•deen] *n*
The house does not have a **garden**.	La casa no tiene **jardín**.
to go up *v*	**subir** [soo•beer] *v*
Have you already **gone up** to the second floor?	¿Ya habéis **subido** al segundo piso?
to have *v*	**tener** [teh•nehr] *v*
Rosa **has** a flat on the beach.	Rosa **tiene** un piso en la playa.
him *pron*	**él** [ehl] *pron m (after prep)*
I have a pressent for **him**.	Tengo un regalo para **él**.
Himself/herself/themselves	**se** [seh] *pron m/f*
My father **shaves** every day.	Mi padre **se** afeita cada día.
The children do not **agree** with one another.	Los niños no **se** acuerdan.

house *n*
*You have a beautiful **house**.*

la casa [lah kah·sah] *n*
*Tenéis una **casa** preciosa.*

key *n*
*I'm looking for the car **key**.*

la llave [la yah·beh] *n*
*Estoy buscando **la llave** del coche.*

kitchen *n*
*My **kitchen** is very big.*

la cocina [lah koh·thee·nah] *n*
*Mi **cocina** es muy grande.*

lift *n*
*The **lift** doesn't work.*

el ascensor [ehl ahs·thehn·sohr] *n*
***El ascensor** no funciona.*

To look *(appearance) v*
*You **look** tired.*

parecer [pah·reh·thehr] *v*
***Pareces** cansada.*

my
*I still haven't combed **my** hair.*

me [meh] *pron m/f*
*Todavía no **me** he peinado.*

nobody/no-one *pron*
*There's **nobody** in the room.*

nadie [nah·deeyeh] *pron*
*No hay **nadie** en la habitación.*

to rent *v*
*I have **rented** a car.*
*Flat for **rent**.*

alquilar [ahl·kee·lahr] *v*
*He **alquilado** un coche.*
*Se **alquila** piso.*

room *n*

*There are no **rooms** vacant in the hotel.*

la habitación
[lah ah·bee·tah·theeyohn] *n*
*En el hotel ya no hay **habitaciones** libres.*

shower *n*
*I'm looking for a room with a **shower**.*

la ducha [lah doo·chah] *n*
*Busco una habitación con **ducha**.*

somebody/someone *pron*

alguien [ahl·geeyehn] *pron*

anybody / anyone *pron*
*Is there **anyone** at home?*

¿Hay **alguien** en casa?

---

table *n*
*The food is on the **table**.*

la mesa [lah meh·sah] *n*
*La comida está ya en **la mesa**.*

---

television *n*
*Our **television** is very big.*

la tele [lah teh·leh] *n*
*Nuestra **tele** no es muy grande.*

---

them *pron*
*This present is for **them**.*

ellas [eh·yahs] *pron f pl (after prep)*
*Este regalo es para **ellas**.*

---

thing *n*
*We have lots of **things** to do.*

la cosa [lah koh·sah] *n*
*Tenemos muchas **cosas** que hacer.*

---

us *pron*
*They never invite **us**.*
*They've already sent **us** four letters.*

nos [nohs] *pron m/f pl*
*No **nos** invitan nunca.*
*Ya **nos** han mandado cuatro cartas.*

---

we *pron*

We don't cook at home; our husbands do.

nosotros, -as
[noh·soh·trohs, trahs] *pron pl*
***Nosotras** no cocinamos en casa; eso lo hacen nuestros maridos.*

We/us
We still haven't gone to bed.

nos [nohs] *pron m/f pl*
*Todavía no **nos** hemos acostado. (acostarse)*

---

wardrobe *n*
*Tomorrow we're going to buy a **wardrobe** for the clothes.*

el armario [ehl ahr·mah·reeyoh] *n*
*Mañana vamos a comprar un **armario** para la ropa.*

---

window *n*
*Open the **window** please.*

la ventana [lah behn·tah·nah] *n*
*Abra **la ventana**, por favor.*

Daily Routine

to be v
Pepito **is** sick.

estar [ehs•tahr] v
Pepito **está** enfermo.

to be v
I am a doctor.

ser [sehr] v
Soy médico.

Fact

Ser is usually used to express the notion of existence: it is used to define people and things, to describe their inherent characteristics and often refer to traits that are permanent, though this is not necessarily always the case. We therefore use the verb **ser** when talking about identity, nationality, profession, and the shape and color of materials.

to be v
I'll **be** at home tomorrow.
What **are** you doing with those scissors?
The children **are** playing in the garden.

estar [ehs•tahr] v
Mañana voy a **estar** en casa.
¿Qué **estás** haciendo con estas tijeras?
Los niños **están** jugando en el jardín.

to change v
Why did they **change** the departure time?

cambiar [kahm•beeyahr] v
¿Por qué se ha **cambiado** la hora de salida?

to close v
Close the door please.

cerrar [theh•rrahr] v
Cierra la puerta, por favor.

to come v
My daughter is **coming** at eight.

venir [beh•neer] v
Mi hija **viene** a las ocho.

to do / make *v*
*What are we **doing** today?*

hacer [ah·thehr] *v*
*¿Qué **hacemos** hoy?*

to go down *v*
*I'm **going down** the town.*
*The price of bread has **gone down**.*

bajar [bah·khahr] *v*
*Voy a **bajar** al pueblo.*
*El precio del pan ha **bajado**.*

to be enough *v*
*It's not **enough** to live on.*

bastar [bahs·tahr] *v*
*No **basta** para vivir.*

to find *v*
*It's difficult **to find** work.*

encontrar [ehn·kohn·trahr] *v*
*Es difícil **encontrar** trabajo.*

to forget *v*
*I have **forgotten** your name.*

olvidar [ohl·bee·dahr] *v*
*He **olvidado** su nombre.*

to get up *v*
*We always **get up** at seven.*

levantarse [leh·bahn·tahr·seh] *v pr*
*Nos **levantamos** siempre a las siete.*

to give *v*
*I'll **give** you my phone number.*

dar [dahr] *v*
*Te **doy** mi número de teléfono.*

to go up *v*
*We **went up** to the top of
the skyscraper.*

*Prices are **going up**.*

subir [soo·beer] *v*
***Subimos** a lo alto del rascacielos.*

*Los precios **suben**.*

to have *v aux*
*Juan **has** eaten a lot.*
***Is** there beer in the fridge?*
*There **is** no one at home.*

haber [ah·behr] *v aux*
*Juan **ha** comido mucho.*
*¿**Hay** cerveza en la nevera?*
*No **hay** nadie en casa.*

to have to
*We **have to** wait a while.*

hay que [aye keh] *locution*
***Hay que** esperar un poco.*

home *n*
*We're going **home**.*

a casa [ah kah·sah] *locution*
*Vamos a **casa**.*

| at home | en casa [ehn kah·sah] *locution* |
| *Juan is not **at home**.* | *Juan no está **en casa**.* |

Fact

The preposition **a** is used when preceded by a verb of motion; however, if you are simply referring to the situation or position of something of someone, you use the preposition **en**.

to leave *v*	quitar [kee·tahr] *v*
Get out of here!	*¡**Quita** los pies de ahí!*
*I **left** my bag behind.*	*¡Me han **quitado** el bolso!*
life *n*	la vida [lah bee·dah] *n*
*That's **life**!*	*¡Así es **la vida**!*
to live *v*	vivir [bee·beer] *v*
*I **live** in Madrid.*	***Vivo** a Madrid.*
to lose *v*	perder [pehr·dehr] *v*
*I have **lost** the money.*	*He **perdido** el dinero.*
noise *n*	el ruido [ehl rooee·doh] *n*
*I can't sleep with this **noise**.*	*No puedo dormir con este **ruido**.*
to look for *v*	buscar [boos·kahr] *v*
*I am **looking** for work in Spain.*	***Busco** trabajo en España.*
nap	la siesta [lah see·es·ta] *n*
*Are they closed for **siesta**?*	*¿Están cerrados a la hora de la **siesta**?*
to need *v*	necesitar [neh·theh·see·tahr] *v*
*Do you **need** something?*	*¿**Necesita** usted algo?*

Fact

The **siesta** is a nap taken after lunch in the early afternoon. This is a common tradition in Spain and Latin America. Be warned, during this time most businesses will close, and many will open again late afternoon, usually after 5:00 p.m.

to open v
*Can I **open** the window?*

abrir [ah•breer] v
*¿Te molesta si **abro** la ventana?*

to pass by v
*On the way back, we will **pass by** Irun.*

pasar [pah•sahr] v
*A la vuelta **pasaremos** por Irún.*

to prepare v
Eva and Ramon have already made dinner.
*We are **preparing** the Birthday party.*

preparar [preh•pah•rahr] v
*Eva y Ramón ya han **preparado** la comida.*
***Preparamos** la fiesta de cumplea ños.*

to put v
*I have **put** the bags in the car.*

meter [meh•tehr] v
*He **metido** las bolsas en el coche.*

repair v
*I think that Ican **repair** the car here.*

arreglar [ah•rreh•glahr] v
*Creo que me pueden **arreglar** el coche aquí.*

to receive v
*We **received** a letter from Julia.*

recibir [reh•thee•beer] v
*Hemos **recibido** una carta de Julia.*

to return / come back v
*They never **get back** before 6p.m.*
*We will **return** next year.*

volver [bohl•behr] v
*Nunca **vuelven** antes de las seis.*
***Volveremos** el año que viene.*

to sit down v Would you like to **sit down**?	**sentarse** [sehn·tahr·seh] v pr ¿Se quiere usted **sentar**?
to sleep v Did you **sleep** well?	**dormir** [dohr·meer] v ¿Has **dormido** bien?
to go to sleep v The baby went **to sleep** straight away.	**dormirse** [dohr·meer·seh] v pr El bebé se ha **dormido** enseguida.
to start v The film **starts** at eight.	**empezar** [ehm·peh·thahr] v La película **empieza** a las ocho.
to stay v My sister will **stay** for five days in our house.	**quedarse** [keh·dahr·seh] v pr Mi hermana se **quedará** cinco días en nuestra casa.
to stop v My father has **stopped** smoking.	**dejar de** [deh·khahr deh] v + inf Mi padre ha **dejado** de fumar.
to take v **Take** my bag please.	**coger** [koh·khehr] v **Coja** mi maleta, por favor.
together adj We'll go to the cinema **together**.	**juntos, -as** [khoon·tohs,tahs] adj Vamos **juntos** al cine.

Fact

The verb **coger** meaning 'to take' can only be used in Castilian, so in Spanish from Spain. In Spanish-speaking countries in South America, you would use **tomar** or **agarrar** to say 'to take' as **coger** has a vulgar connotation!

to touch v
Don't **touch** the flowers!

tocar [toh·kahr] v
¡No **toques** las flores!

to turn on v
Can you **turn on** the light please?

encender [ehn·thehn·dehr] v
¿Podrías **encender** la luz, por favor?

to wash v
I need to **wash** these trousers.

lavar [lah·bahr] v
Tengo que **lavar** estos pantalones.

to work / operate v
The air conditioning does not **work**.

funcionar [foon·thee·oh·nahr] v
El aire acondicionado no **funciona**.

Clothes & Accessories

blouse n
Do you like my **blouse**?

la blusa [lah bloo·sah] n
¿Te gusta mi **blusa**?

coat n
I bought myself a new **coat**.

el abrigo [ehl ah·bree·goh] n
Me he comprado un **abrigo** nuevo.

clothing n
The children need summer **clothes**.

la ropa [la roh·pah] n
Los niños necesitan **ropa** de verano.

glasses n pl
How long have you worn **glasses** for?

las gafas [lahs gah·fahs] n pl
¿Desde cuándo llevas **gafas**?

Hot adj
It's **hot**. Why don't you take off your sweater?

calor [kah·lohr] adj
Hace **calor**. – ¿Por qué no te quitas el jersey?

jacket n
I need a summer **jacket**.

la chaqueta [lah chah·keh·tah] n
Necesito una **chaqueta** de verano.

outfit *n*
*You are wearing a very nice **outfit**.*

el vestido [ehl behs·tee·doh] *n*
*Llevas un **vestido** muy bonito.*

- -

to put on *v*
*The girl does not want to **put on** the sweater.*

ponerse [poh·nehr·seh] *v pr*
*La niña no quiere **ponerse** el jersey.*

- -

shirt *n*
*Your **shirt** is dirty.*

la camisa [lah kah·mee·sah] *n*
*Tu **camisa** está sucia.*

- -

shoe *n*
*These **shoes** are pinching me.*

el zapato [ehl thah·pah·toh] *n*
*Estos **zapatos** me aprietan.*

- -

skirt *n*
*Have you seen my red **skirt**?*

la falda [lah fahl·dah] *n*
*¿Has visto mi **falda** roja?*

- -

sweater *n*
*I'll take this **sweater**.*

el jersey [ehl khehr·sehee] *n*
*Me llevo este **jersey**.*

- -

t-shirt *n*
*I put three **t-shirts** in the suitcase.*

la camiseta [lah kah·mee·seh·tah] *n*
*He metido tres **camisetas** en la maleta.*

- -

to take off *v*

quitarse [kee·tahr·seh] *v pr*

- -

this *pron*
*Where did you buy **this**?*

esto [ehs·toh] *pron n, cf. Este*
*¿Dónde has comprado **esto**?*

- -

tights *n pl*
*I need black **tights**.*

las medias [lahs meh·deeyahs] *n pl*
*Necesito **medias** negras.*

- -

trousers *n pl*

*The **trousers** are blue.*

el pantalón (pl los pantalones)
[ehl pahn·tah·lohn] *n*
*El **pantalón** es azul.*

- -

to try on *v*
*Can I **try on** this sweater.*

probarse [proh·bahr·seh] *v pr*
*¿Puedo **probarme** este jersey?*

Fact

Pantalon (sing.) and **pantalones** (plur) can be used interchangeably to refer to 'trousers'.

On the Move

airport *n*

Shall I drive you to the **airport** in my car?

el aeropuerto
[ehl aheh·roh·poo·ehr·toh] *n*
¿Le llevo en mi coche al **aeropuerto**?

to arrive *v*
The train hasn't **arrived** yet.

llegar [yeh·gahr] *v*
El tren no ha **llegado** todavía.

arrival *n*
Do you know the **arrival** time yet?

la llegada [lah yeh·gah·dah] *n*
¿Sabes ya la hora de **llegada**?

bus *n*
We're going by **bus** aren't we?

el autobús [ehl aw·toh·boos] *n*
Vamos en **autobús**, ¿no?

(bus) stop *n*
We're looking for the **(bus) stop**.

la parada [lah pah·rah·dah] *n*
Estamos buscando **la parada**.

car *n*
The **car** has four doors.

el coche [ehl koh·cheh] *n*
El coche tiene cuatro puertas.

center *n*
You can park in the **centre**.

el centro [ehl thehn·troh] *n*
En **el centro** no se puede aparcar.

to change *v*
Let's go by bus, so we don't have to **change**.

cambiar [kahm·beeyahr] *v*
Vamos en autobús, así no necesitamos **cambiar**.

departure *n*
They've changed the **departure** time.

la salida [lah sah·lee·dah] *n*
Han cambiado la hora de **la salida**.

---

to depart *v*
to leave *v*
The train **leaves** at seven.
The plane **leaves** at seven.

salir [sah·leer] *v*

El tren **sale** a las siete.
El avión **sale** a las siete.

---

drive *v*
Do you know how to **drive**?

conducir [kohn·doo·theer] *v*
¿Sabes **conducir**?

---

to fix *v*
They still have not **fixed** the car.

reparar [reh·pah·rahr] *v*
Todavía no han **reparado** el coche.

---

to fly *v*
In this area planes **fly** very low.

volar [boh·lahr] *v*
En esta zona los aviones **vuelan** muy bajo.

---

for *prep*
The train **for** Guadalajara leaves at 10:00a.m.

para [pah·rah] *prep*
El tren **para** Guadalajara sale a las diez.

---

to get off *v*
Get off at the next stop.

bajar [bah·khahr] *v*
Baje usted en la próxima parada.

---

to get on
I **got on** at the first stop.

subir [soo·beer] *v*
He **subido** en la primera parada.

---

to go *v*
Martha always **goes** to work by car.

ir [eer] *v*
Marta siempre **va** al trabajo en coche.

---

to go (away) *v*
to leave *v*
I have to **leave**, goodbye.

irse [eer·seh] *v pr*

Tengo que **irme**, adiós.

to go on foot *locution* Why don't we go **on foot**?	**ir a pie** [eer a peeyeh] *locution* ¿Por qué no vamos **a pie**?
to go out *v* When it's cold I don't like to **go out**.	**salir** [sah·leer] *v* Cuando hace frío, no me gusta **salir**.
late *adv* It's already **late**.	**tarde** [tahr·deh] *adv* Ya es **tarde**.
to take / bring *v* The bus will **take** you to the center. Can you **bring** music to the party?	**llevar** [yeh·bahr] *v* El autobús le **lleva** hasta el centro. ¿Puedes **llevar** música a la fiesta?
to miss *v* We're going **to miss** the plane.	**perder** [pehr·dehr] *v* Vamos a **perder** el avión.
motorway *n* The new **motorway** cost a lot of money.	**la autopista** [lah aw·toh·pees·tah] *n* La nueva **autopista** ha costado mucho dinero.
oil *n* I need to check the **oil** level before leaving.	**el aceite** [ehl ah·thehee·teh] *n* Tengo que comprobar el nivel de **aceite** antes de arrancar.
on time *adv* I want to arrive **on time**.	**a tiempo** [ah teeyehm·poh] *adv* Quiero llegar **a tiempo**.
to pass through *v* The plane **passes through** Ibiza.	**pasar por** [pah·sahr pohr] *v* El avión **pasa por** Ibiza.
to park *v* You can't **park** here.	**aparcar** [ah·pahr·kahr] *v* Aquí no se puede **aparcar**.

Fact

The verb **pasar** can mean 'to pass through' but also as 'to come in' **(pase usted)** and expresses an idea of movement, of passing from one place to another.

to pass through *v*	**pasar por** [pah•sahr pohr] *v*
The coach **passes through** *Madrid.*	*El autocar* **pasa por** *Madrid.*
plane *n*	**el avión** [ehl ah•beeyohn] *n*
We're taking the **plane**.	*Tomaremos* **el avión**.
road *n*	**la carretera** [lah kah•rreh•teh•rah] *n*
I didn't find the **road** *to Granada.*	*No he encontrado* **la carretera** *a Granada.*
service station *n*	**la estación de servicio** [lah ehs•tah•theeyohn deh sehr•bee•theeyoh] *n*
The **service station** *is closed.*	*La estación de servicio* *está cerrada.*
site *n*	**el sitio** [ehl see•teeyoh] *n*
This is a big tourist **site**.	*Es un* **sitio** *muy turístico.*
station *n*	**la estación** [lah ehs•tah•theeyohn] *n*
Where's the central **station**?	*¿Dónde está* **la estación** *central?*
still *adv*	**todavía** [toh•dah•bee•ah] *adv*
There's **still** *time.*	*Todavía hay tiempo.*

to stop v The bus doesn't **stop** here.	**parar** [pah·rahr] v El autobús no **para** aquí.
street n It is a very quiet **street**.	**la calle** [lah kah·yeh] n Es una **calle** muy tranquila.
to take v I'll **take** the suitcase, you **take** the bag	**tomar** [toh·mahr] v Yo **tomo** la maleta, **tome** usted la bolsa.
taxi n There are no free **taxis**.	**el taxi** [ehl tah·xee] n No hay **taxis** libres.
through prep The bus goes **through** the center.	**por** [pohr] prep El autobús pasa **por** el centro.
ticket n We still haven't bought our train **tickets**. **Tickets** for the underground are very expensive.	**el billete** [ehl bee·yeh·teh] n Todavía no hemos comprado los **billetes** de tren. El **billete** de metro es muy caro.
time n They've changed the departure **time**.	**la hora** [lah oh·rah] n Han cambiado la **hora** de salida.
traffic n There is always a lot of **traffic** here.	**el tráfico** [ehl trah·fee·koh] n Aquí siempre hay mucho **tráfico**.
train n The **train** leaves at one.	**el tren** [ehl trehn] n **El tren** sale a la una.
to go by train locution I prefer **to go by train**.	**ir en tren** [eer ehn trehn] loc Prefiero **ir en tren**.

underground n	**el metro** [ehl meh·troh] n
I go to work by **underground**.	Voy en **metro** al trabajo.
to wait for v	**esperar** [ehs·peh·rahr] v
We will **wait for** you at the station.	Te esperamos en la **estación**.

Asking for Directions

Fact

Ir en is always used with a means of transport: **ir en coche**, **ir en autobús**. One exception however is 'to go on foot' which is **ir a pie**.

another adj	**otro, -a** [oh·troh, trah] pron
I think the cinema is in **another** street.	Creo que el cine está en **otra** calle.
East n	**el Este** [ehl ehs·teh] n
The sun rises in the **East**.	El Sol sale por **el Este**.
East adv	**al este de** [ahl ehs·teh deh] prep
East of Valencia are the las Balearic Islands.	**Al este de** Valencia se encuentran Islas Baleares.
in front of prep	**delante de** [deh·lahn·teh deh] prep
We parked the car **in front** of the hotel	Hemos aparcado el coche **delante** del hotel.

kilometer n	**el quilómetro** [ehl kee·loh·meh·troh] n
Bilbao is 30 **kilometers** away.	Bilbao está a treinta **quilómetros**.
know v	**saber** [sah·behr] v
I **know** how to count to 100 in German.	**Sé** contar hasta cien en alemán.
metre n	**el metro** [ehl meh·troh] n
The bus stop is a 100 **metres** from here.	La parada está a cien **metros** de aquí.
next to prep	**al lado de** [al lah·doh] prep
There's a restaurant **next to** museum.	**Al lado** del museo hay un the restaurante.
North n	**el Norte** [ehl nohr·teh] n
The **North** of Spain is quite cold.	**El Norte** de España es bastante frío.
North adv	**al norte de** [ahl nohr·teh deh] prep
It's **North** of Madrid.	Está **al norte de** Madrid.
on the right locution	**a la derecha** [ah lah deh·reh·chah] locution
There's a bar on the **right**.	**A la derecha** hay un bar.
on the left locution	**a la izquierda** [ah lah eeth·keeyehr·dah] locution
Can you see the girl **on the left**?	¿Ves a la chica que está **a la izquierda**?
South n	**el Sur** [el 'sur] n
Sandra would like to travel around **South** Chile.	Sandra quiere recorrer **el Sur** de Chile.

South adv Tierra del Fuega is **South** of Arfentina and Chile.	**al sur de** [ahl soor deh] prep La Tierra del Fuego está **al sur de** Argentina y Chile.
straight adv Continue **straight** ahead.	**recto** [rehk·toh] adv Siga usted todo **recto**.
to There's a pharmacy 100 metres from here	**a** [ah] prep **A** cien metros de aquí hay una farmacia.
to prep We're going **to** Madrid.	**a** [ah] prep Vamos **a** Madrid.
to prep The bus takes you **to** the station.	**hasta** [ahs·tah] prep El autobús le lleva **hasta** la estación.
traffic lights n Can you see the **traffic lights**? The museum is there.	**el semáforo** [ehl seh·mah·foh·roh] n ¿Ve **el semáforo**? Allí está el museo.
West n We live in the **West**, not in the center.	**el Oeste** [ehl oh·ehs·teh] n Nosotros vivimos en **el Oeste**, no en el centro.
West adv Portugal is to the **West** of Spain.	**al oeste de** [ahl oh·ehs·teh deh] prep **Al oeste** de España está Portugal.

already *adv*
I've **already** spoken to her.

ya [yah] *adv*
Ya he hablado con ella.

always *adv*
He **always** comes at this time.

siempre [seeyehm·preh] *adv*
Siempre viene a esta hora.

at *prep*
My friends are **at** the beach.

en [ehn] *prep*
Mis amigos están **en** la playa.

to believe / think *v*
Do you believe in astrology?
I **think** I made a mistake.
It's an easy question, don't
you think?

creer [kreh·ehr] *v*
¿**Crees** en la astrología?
Creo que me he equivocado.
Es una pregunta fácil, ¿no **crees**?

difficult *adj*

This task is very **difficult**.

difícil (pl difíciles)
[dee·fee·theel] *adj*
Esta tarea es muy **difícil**.

easy *adj*
It's **easy** to find the museum.

fácil (pl fáciles) [fah·theel] *adj*
Es **fácil** encontrar el museo.

for *prep*
This book is **for** you.

para [pah·rah] *prep*
Este libro es **para** ti.

him/her/you/it
What should I say to **him**?
Give **him** the book.

le [leh] *pron m/f*
¿Qué **le** digo?
Da**le** el libro.

Him, her, you, they
How do **you** do this?

se [seh] *pron*
¿Cómo **se** hace esto?

in *prep*
Explain it **in** Spanish.

en [ehn] *prep*
Explícalo **en** español.

71

*We're going **in** the car, aren't we?*   *Vamos **en** coche, ¿no?*
*They live **in** Mallorca.*   *Viven **en** Mallorca.*
*Juan is **in** Seville.*   *Juan está **en** Sevilla.*

to inform *v*   **informar** [een·fohr·mahr] *v*
*Nobody **informed** us of this change.*   *Nadie nos ha **informado** de este cambio.*
*Can you **tell us** the timetable?*   *¿Nos puede **informar** sobre los horarios?*

to interest *v*   **interesar** [een·teh·reh·sahr] *v*
*This film **interests** me.*   *Me **interesa** mucho esta película.*

interesting *adj*   **interesante** [een·teh·reh·sahn·teh] *adj*
*It is a very **interesting** book.*   *Es un libro muy **interesante**.*

to know (person/place) *v*   **conocer** [koh·noh·ther] *v*
*I don't **know** Maria.*   *Yo no **conozco** a Maria.*

to know (fact) *v*   **saber** [sah·behr] *v*
*I don't **know**.*   *No lo sé.*
*The little girl already **knows** how to read.*   *La niña ya **sabe** leer.*

Fact

The verb **conocer** is used when knowing a person or a place. For a person, **conocer** is always followed by **'a'** — **concocer a** + person. When saying you know a place, you use **conocer** alone e.g. I know London — **Yo conozco Londres**. For how to say you have knowledge of something and know facts, see **saber** on page 69.

to learn *v*	**aprender** [ah·prehn·dehr] *v*
I would like to **learn** Spanish.	Quiero **aprender** español.
to leave *v*	**dejar** [deh·khahr] *v*
You don't let me speak!	¡No me **dejas** hablar!
Will you **leave** me your pen?	¿Me **dejas** tu bolígrafo?
to make a mistake *v*	**equivocarse** [eh·kee·boh·kahr·seh] *v pr*
Sorry, I **made a mistake**.	Perdón, me he **equivocado**.
never *adv*	**nunca** [nuhn·kah] *adv*
He **never** writes.	No escribe **nunca**.
no longer *locution*	**ya no** [yah noh] *adv*
It **no longer** interests me.	**Ya no** me interesa.
of	**de** [deh] *prep*
It's not Pilar's car.	No es el coche **de** Pilar.
on *prep*	**en** [ehn] *prep*
There's a book for you **on** the table.	**En** la mesa hay un libro para ti.
paper *n*	**el papel (pl los papeles)** [ehl pah·pehl] *n*
I need **paper** to write a letter.	Necesito **papel** para escribir una carta.
pen *n*	**el bolígrafo** [ehl boh·lee·grah·foh] *n* *abbr* **el boli**
Can you lend me your **pen** a minute please?	¿Me prestas un momento tu **bolígrafo**?

to permit
Can I ask you a question?

permitir [pehr•mee•teer] *v*
*¿Me **permite** usted una pregunta?*

Primary school *n*
*The children go to **school**.*

la escuela [lah ehs•koo•eh•lah] *n*
*Los niños van a **la escuela**.*

---

to put *v*
*Can you **put** the books on the table.*

poner [poh•nehr] *v*
*Puedes **poner** los libros en la mesa.*

Secondary school *n*
***Secondary school** starts in September.*

el colegio [ehl koh•leh•geeoh] *n*
***El colegio** empieza en septiembre.*

---

solution *n*

la solución
[lah soh•loo•theeyohn] *n*

*It's not easy to find a **solution**.*

*No es fácil encontrar una **solución**.*

---

student *n*
*There are fifteen **students** in the class.*

el alumno [ehl ah•loom•noh] *n*
*Hay quince **alumnos** en la clase.*

la alumna [lah ah•loom•nah] *n*
(female student)

*Ana is the oldest **student**.*

*Ana es la mejor **alumna**.*

---

student *n*

el estudiante
[ehl ehs•too•deeahn•teh] *n*

*Lots of **students** live here.*

Aquí viven muchos estudiantes.

la estudiante
[lah ehs•too•deeahn•teh] *n*

*The new teacher is nice to the **students**.*

*El nuevo profesor es simpático con **las estudiantes**.*

---

to study *v*
I need to **study** more.
Carlos **studies** several languages.

estudiar [ehs·too·deeyahr] *v*
Tengo que **estudiar** más.
Carlos **estudia** varios idiomas.

---

to teach *v*
Pedro has **taught** me some
swearwords in Spanish.

enseñar [ehn·seh·nyahr] *v*
Pedro me ha **enseñado** algunas
palabrotas en español.

---

teacher *m n*
Our **teacher** is from Chile.

el profesor [ehl proh·feh·sohr] *n*
Nuestro **profesor** es de Chile.

---

teacher *f n*

My mother is a **teacher**.

la profesora
[lah proh·feh·soh·rah] *n*
Mi madre es **profesora**.

---

that *pron*
The book **that** you're looking for
is on the table.

que [keh] *pron m/f*
El libro **que** buscas está en la mesa.

---

to *prep*
I need some money **to** buy a car.

para [pah·rah] *prep*
Necesito el dinero **para** comprar
un coche.

---

to *prep*
I don't know Pedro.
I gave the book **to** Juan.

a [ah] *prep*
Yo no conozco **a** Pedro.
He dado el libro **a** Juan.

---

until *prep*
I work **until** six.

hasta [ahs·tah] *prep*
Trabajo **hasta** las seis.

---

you *pron pl*

Laura and Teresa, can **you**
a little longer?

vosotros, -as
[boh·soh·trohs, trahs] *pron pl*
¿Laura y Teresa, **vosotras** os
quedáis un poco más?

to write *v*
Carlos already knows how
to **write**.

escribir [ehs•kree•beer] *v*
Carlos ya sabe **escribir**.

Official Business

to appear/seem *v*
There **seems** to have been a
misunderstanding.
You **seem** tired.
What do you make of this town?

parecer [pah•reh•ther] *v*
Me **parece** que hay un
malentendido.
Pareces cansado.
¿Qué le **parece** este pueblo?

Fact

El banco is used to depict the banking establishment whereas **la banca** refers to the banking sector.

bank *n*
I'm looking for a **bank** to change
some money.

el banco [ehl bahn•koh] *n*
Busco un **banco** para cambiar
dinero.

because *conj*
I'm still at the office **because** I
have a lot of work.

porque [pohr•keh] *conj*
Me quedo en la oficina **porque**
tengo mucho trabajo.

boss *n*

What time does the **boss**
come in?

el jefe [ehl kheh•feh] *m n*
la jefa [lah kheh•fah] *f n*
¿A qué hora viene **el jefe**?

calm *adj*

tranquilo, -a
[trahn•kee•loh,lah] *adj*

*Can you remain **calm**, Mr Mendez.* *Puede usted estar **tranquilo**, señor Méndez.*

---

to change *v*

cambiar [kahm•beeyahr] *v*

*We have to **change** some money.* *Tenemos que **cambiar** dinero.*

---

check *n*

el cheque [ehl cheh•keh] *n*

*Can I also pay by **check**?* *¿También puedo pagar con **cheque**?*

---

consulate *n*

el consulado
[ehl kohn•soo•lah•doh] *n*

*I have to get in touch with the **consulate**.* *Tengo que ponerme en contacto con **el consulado**.*

---

credit card *n*

la tarjeta de crédito
[lah tahr•kheh•tah deh kreh•dee•toh] *n*

*Here's my **credit card**.* *Aquí tiene mi **tarjeta de crédito**.*

---

to earn *v*

ganar [gah•nahr] *v*

*How much do you **earn** a month?* *¿Cuánto **ganas** al mes?*

---

embassy *n*

la embajada
[lah ehm•bah•khah•dah] *n*

*We're looking for the French **embassy**.* *Buscamos **la embajada** francesa.*

---

employee *n*

el empleado
[ehl ehm•pleh•ahdoh] *m n*
la empleada
[lah ehm•pleh•ahdah] *f n*

*I met the new **employee** today.* *Hoy he conocido a la nueva **empleada**.*

the factory n
*There are lots of **factories** in this city.*

la fábrica [lah fah·bree·kah] n
*En esta ciudad hay muchas **fábricas.***

to fill in v
*Please could you **fill in** this form?*

rellenar [rreh·yeh·nahr] v
*Por favor, **rellene** este impreso.*

to forbid v
*My mother **forbids** me to smoke.
Parking is **forbidden**.*

prohibir [proh·ee·beer] v
*Mi madre me **prohibe** fumar.
Prohibido aparcar.*

form n
*We have to fill in the **form**.*

el impreso [ehl eem·preh·soh] n
*Tenemos que rellenar **el impreso**.*

to help v
*Can I **help** you?*

ayudar [ah·yoo·dahr] v
*¿Quieres que te **ayude**?*

her pron
*I don't know **her**.*

la [lah] pron f
*No **la** conozco.*

industry n

*In this region there is a lot of **industry**.*

la industria
[lah een·doos·treeyah] n
*En esta región hay muchas **industrias**.*

insurance n
*I pay for the car **insurance** every six months.*

el seguro [ehl seh·goo·roh] n
*Pago **el seguro** del coche cada seis meses.*

library n

*I'm sure you can find that book in the **library**.*

la biblioteca
[lah bee·bleeyoh·teh·kah] n
*Seguro que encuentras ese libro en **la biblioteca**.*

money *n*	**el dinero** [ehl dee·neh·roh] *n*
Do you need **money**?	¿Necesitas **dinero**?
not *adv*	**no** [noh] *adv*
I'm **not** working today.	Hoy **no** trabajo.
office *n*	**la oficina** [la oh·fee·thee·nah] *n*
The **office** is closed.	**La oficina** está cerrada.
on *prep*	**sobre** [soh·breh] *prep*
It was a conference **on** the environment.	Fui a una conferencia **sobre** el medioambiente.
The letters are **on** the table.	Las cartas están **sobre** la mesa.

partner *n*	**el compañero** [ehl kohm·pah·nyeh·roh] *m n*
	la compañera [lah kohm·pah·nyeh·rah] *f n*
My **partner** has gone on holidays.	Mi **compañera** se ha ido de vacaciones.
post office *n*	***la oficina de correos*** [lah oh·fee·thee·nah] *n* – abbr correos
The **post office** is already closed.	La **oficina de correos** ya está cerrada.

Fact

If you are going to the post office you would normally just say **Voy a correos**, shortening the official term **oficina de correos** to 'correos'.

police n
We have already spoken to the **police**.

la policía [lah poh·lee·theeyah] n
Ya hemos hablado con **la policía**.

---

to promise v
I **promise** to find a solution.

prometer [proh·meh·tehr] v
Le **prometo** buscar una solución.

---

to see v
I can't **see** well without glasses.

ver [behr] v
No **veo** bien sin gafas.

---

signature n
The letter arrived with no **signature**.

la firma [lah feer·mah] n
La carta ha llegado sin **firma**.

---

to spend v
Pedro **spends** all the money he earns.

gastar [gahs·tahr] v
Pedro **gasta** todo el dinero que gana.

---

that's why locution
That's why I can't help you.

por eso [pohr eh·soh] adv
Por eso no te puedo ayudar.

---

them pron
Do you know these girls? - No, I don't know **them**.

las [lahs] pron f pl
¿Conoces a estas chicas? – No, no **las** conozco.

---

them pron
I haven't seen **them**.

las [lahs] pron f pl
No **las** he visto.

---

them pron
Do you know those men? - No, I don't know **them**.

los [lohs] pron m pl, cf. lo
¿Conoces a estos hombres? – No, no **los** conozco.

---

to think v
What are you **thinking**?

pensar [pehn·sahr] v
¿Qué estás **pensando**?

---

to touch v
Do not **touch**!

tocar [toh·kahr] v
¡No **tocar**!

Don't **touch** that!	¡No **toques** eso!
town/city council n	**el ayuntamiento** [ehl ah•yoon•tah•meeyehn•toh] n
The **city council** wants to to build a new car park.	**El ayuntamiento** quiere construir un nuevo aparcamiento.
to wait v	**esperar** [ehs•peh•rahr] v
Wait a moment please.	**Espera** un momento, por favor.
to watch v	**ver** [behr] v
Last night I stayed in **watching** television.	Anoche me quedé en casa **viendo** la tele.
you pron pl (polite form)	**los** [lohs] pron m pl
I have never seen **you** here before.	A ustedes nunca **los** he visto antes por aquí.
you pron pl (polite form)	**les** [lehs] pron m/f pl
Would you like us to help **you**?	¿Quieren que **les** ayudemos?
you pron sg (polite form)	**lo** [loh] pron m
I don't know **you**.	A usted no **lo** conozco.
work / job n	**el trabajo** [ehl trah•bah•khoh] n
It's a very interesting **job**.	Es un **trabajo** muy interesante.
to work v	**trabajar** [trah•bah•khahr] v
Are you not **working** today?	¿No **trabajas** hoy?
workman n	**el obrero** [ehl oh•breh•roh] n m **la obrera** [lah oh•breh•rah] n f
I'm a **workman**.	Soy **obrero**.
workshop n	**el taller** [ehl tah•yehr] n
We took the car to the **workshop**.	Hemos llevado el coche al **taller**.

Communicating

and conj
Pedro **and** Teresa are going to Cordoba.

y [ee] conj
Pedro **y** Teresa van a Córdoba.

. . . .

to call v
I'll **call** the children and we can eat.

llamar [yah•mahr] v
Llamo a los niños y vamos a comer.

. . . .

to call oneself v
What is your name?

llamarse [yah•mahr•seh] v pr
¿Cómo se **llama** usted?

. . . .

to call on the phone v

Call me as soon as you can.

llamar (por teléfono)
[yah•mahr (pohr teh•leh•foh•noh)] v
Llámame tan pronto como puedas.

. . . .

to chat v
My daughter spends hours upon hours **chatting** with her friends.

charlar [chahr•lahr] v
Mi hija se pasa horas y horas **charlando** con sus amigos.

. . . .

computer n

My **computer** is very powerful.

el ordenador
[ehl ohr•deh•nah•dohr] n
Mi **ordenador** es muy potente.

. . . .

dear adj

Dear Mr. Alvarez (formal)

Dear Maria (informal)

estimado, -a
[ehs•tee•mah•doh,dah] adj
Estimado Señor Álvarez:
querido, -a
[keh•ree•doh, dah] adj
Querido Maria, . . .

. . . .

e-mail n

I ordered it by **e-mail**.

el correo electrónico [ehl
koh•rreh•oh eh•lehk•troh•nee•koh] n
Se lo mando por **correo
electronico**.

. . . .

Excuse me? *transitive verb* **Excuse me**, can you help me?	**perdón** [pehr•dohn] *interj* **Perdón**, ¿me puede ayudar?
to explain *v* Can you **explain** this to me?	**explicar** [ex•plee•kahr] *v* ¿Me puede **explicar** esto?
film *n* It is one of the best **films** I have seen.	**la película** [lah peh•lee•koo•lah] *n* Es una de las mejores **películas** que he visto.
good *adj* It's okay.	**bien** [beeyehn] *adv* Está **bien**.
good afternoon **Good afternoon**, we have reserved a table.	**Buenas tardes.** [booeh•nahs tahr•dehs] *locution* **Buenas tardes**, hemos reservado una mesa.

Fact

In Spanish you use the greeting **Buenas tardes** in the early afternoon (from about 2:00 p.m.) until it gets dark. It can therefore be translated as 'good afternoon' as well as 'good evening' depending on the time of day.

goodbye **Goodbye**, see you tomorrow.	**adiós** [ah•deeyohs] *interj* **Adiós**, nos vemos mañana.
good night We're off, **good night**.	**Buenas noches.** [booeh•nahs noh•chehs] *locution* Nos vamos, **buenas noches**.

Fact

In Spain you use the greeting **Buenas noches** as soon as it starts getting dark. You also use this form to say good night just before going to bed.

to greet/say hello to *v* *I'm going to **say hello** to your parents.*	**saludar** [sah·loo·dahr] *v* *Voy a **saludar** a tus padres.*
to have to *v* *Bye! I **have to** go.*	**tener que** [teh·nehr keh] *locution + inf* *¡Adiós! **Tengo** que irme*
hello *Hello, can I have a coffee please.*	**¡Buenos días!** [booeh·nohs deeyahs] *locution* ***Buenos días**, un café, por favor.*

Fact

In Spain you use the greeting **Buenos días** until lunch time (about 2:00 p.m.).

Hi! *Hi! How are you?*	**¡Hola!** [oh·lah] *interj* *¡Hola! ¿Cómo estás?*
him *pron* *No, I haven't seen **him**.*	**lo** [loh] *pron m* *No, no **lo** he visto.*
important *adj* *It's a very **important** letter.*	**importante** [eem·pohr·tahn·teh] *adj* *Es una carta muy **importante**.*

information *n*

We need more **information**.

la información
[lah een·fohr·mah·theeyohn] *n*
Necesitamos más **información**.

internet

I found my last job online.

el o la internet [een·tehr·neht] *n*
Encontré mi último trabajo gracias
a **internet**.

isn't it?
It's not as hot today, **is it**?

¿No? [noh] *interj*
Hoy hace menos calor, ¿**no**?

it *pron n*
I don't know.

lo [loh] *pron n*
No **lo** sé.

laptop *n*

I don't have this application
on my **laptop**.

el ordenador portátil [ehl
ohr·deh·nah·dohr pohr·tah·teel] *n*
No tengo este programa en mi
ordenador portátil.

letter *n*
I received a **letter** from my friend.

la carta [lah kahr·tah] *n*
He recibido una **carta** de un amigo
mío.

to look at *v*
Don't **look at** me like that.

mirar [mee·rahr] *v*
No me **mires** así.

mobile phone *n*

Why don't you call me on
my **mobile**?

el teléfono móvil
[ehl teh·leh·foh·noh moh·beel] *n*
¿Por qué no me llamaste al
teléfono móvil?

neither *adv*
either *adv*
My friend isn't coming **either**.

tampoco [tahm·poh·koh] *adv*

Mi amigo no viene **tampoco**.

newspaper *n*	**el periódico** [ehl peh•ree•oh•dee•koh] *n*
*I always read the **newspaper** going to work.*	*Antes de ir al trabajo siempre leo **el periódico.***
no *adv*	**no** [noh] *adv*
*Do you want a beer? - **No** thanks. I'm not feeling very well.*	*¿Quieres una cerveza? – **No**, gracias. **No** me siento muy bien.*
okay	**bien, …** [beeyehn] *interj*
***Okay**, we can stay at home if you like.*	***Bien**, si quieres, nos quedamos en casa.*
okay	**vale** [bah•leh] *locution*
***Okay**, I'll go with you.*	***Vale**, voy con vosotros.*
to order	**mandar** [mahn•dahr] *v*
*If you would like, I will **order** the book for you.*	*Si quieres, te **mando** el libro.*
please *adv*	**por favor** [pohr fah•bohr] *locution*
***Please**, do it for me.*	***Por favor**, hazlo por mí.*
question *n*	**la pregunta** [lah preh•goon•tah] *n*
*I have a **question** for you.*	*Tengo que hacerle una **pregunta.***
to ask a question *v*	**preguntar** [preh•goon•tahr] *v*
*Your parents didn't **ask** me anything.*	*Tus padres no me han **preguntado** nada.*
radio *n*	**la radio** [lah rah•deeoh] *n*
*I don't like listening to the **radio**.*	*No me gusta oír **la radio.***

to recommend v	**recomendar** [reh·koh·mehn·dahr] v
I **recommend** the daily menu.	Le **recomiendo** el menú del día.
to repeat v	**repetir** [reh·peh·teer] v
I don't want to **repeat** it.	No lo quiero **repetir**.
to reply v	**contestar** [kohn·tehs·tahr] v
Can you **reply** to me this week?	¿Puede usted **contestarme** esta semana?
to reply to v	**contestar** [kohn·tehs·tahr] v
Claudia has still not **replied** to my letter.	Claudia todavía no ha **contestado** a mi carta.
to see v	**ver** [behr] v
I'm pleased to **see** him!	¡Me alegro de **verle**!
to see one another v	**verse** [behr·seh] v pr
Shall we **see one another** on Sunday?	¿Nos **vemos** el domingo?
See you later!	**¡Hasta luego!** [ahs·tah looeh·goh] locution
We have to go. **See you later!**	Tenemos que irnos. **¡Hasta luego!**
situation n	**la situación** [lah see·tooah·theeyohn] n
We are in a difficult **situation**.	Estamos en una **situación** difícil.
to show v	**enseñar** [ehn·seh·nyahr] v
Can you **show** me the room?	¿Me puede **enseñar** la habitación?
Sorry?	**¿Cómo dice?** [koh·moh dee·theh] locution abbr ¿Cómo?

Sorry? *I didn't hear you Mrs Latorre.*	***¿Cómo dice?*** *No la he entendido, señora Latorre.*
to be sorry v ***Sorry*** *to arrive so late.*	**sentir** [sehn·teer] v ***Siento*** *llegar tan tarde.*
I'm sorry. *I'm **sorry** but I already have something planned on Saturday.*	**Lo siento.** [loh seeyehn·toh] *locution* ***Lo siento**, pero el sábado ya tengo algo previsto.*
to speak v *Do you **speak** Spanish?*	**hablar** [ah·blahr] v *¿**Habla** usted español?*
stamp n *Where can I buy **stamps**?*	**el sello** [ehl seh·yoh] n *¿Dónde puedo comprar **sellos**?*
telephone n *Can I fix the **telephone**?*	**el teléfono** [ehl teh·leh·foh·noh] n *¿Me puede reparar **el teléfono**?*
television n *There is an interesting film on **television**.*	**la televisión** [lah teh·leh·bee·see·ohn] n *En **la televisión** hay una película interesante.*
telephone number *What is your **telephone number**?*	**el número** [ehl noo·meh·roh] n *¿Qué **número** de teléfono tiene usted?*
text message n *Why not send me a **text message**?*	**el mensaje de texto** [ehl mehn·sah·kheh deh tehx·toh] n *¿Por qué no me mandas un **mensaje de texto**?*

to tell *v*
Pablo **told** me everything.

contar [kohn·tahr] *v*
Pablo me lo ha **contado** todo.

thank you *locution*
How are you?
Good, **thank you.**

gracias [grah·theeahs] *locution*
¿Cómo está?
– Bien, **gracias.**

Thanks very much.

Thanks very much for
the flowers.

Muchas gracias.
[moo·chahs grah·theeahs] *locution*
Muchas gracias por las flores.

that *conj*
I don't think **that** he is coming.

que [keh] *conj*
No creo **que** viene.

that's right *locution*
That's right!

así [ah·see] *adv*
¡Así es!

them *pron*

It's impossible to talk with **them**.

ellos [eh·yohs]
pron m pl (after prep)
Con **ellos** no se puede hablar.

too *adv*
Me **too!**

también [tahm·beeyehn] *adv*
¡Yo también!

to understand *v*
I don't un**derstand** what you are
trying to tell me, Mr Ramirez.

entender [ehn·tehn·dehr] *v*
No **entiendo** qué quiere decirme,
señor Ramírez.

you're welcome *locution*
Thanks for the books.
– **You're welcome!**

de nada [deh nah·dah] *locution*
¡Gracias por los libros! – **¡De nada!**

What's up?
What's up?

¿Qué pasa? [keh pah·sah] *locution*
¿Qué pasa?

yes *adv*
yes, I'm Argentinian.

sí [see] *adv*
Sí, soy argentina.

you *pron pl (polite form)*

I think this letter is for **you**.
We talked about **you**.

ustedes [oos•teh•dehs] *pron m/f pl (after prep)*
Creo que esta carta es para **ustedes**.
Hemos hablado de **ustedes**.

you *pron pl*

This letter is for **you**.
I'm doing it for **you**.

vosotros, -as
[boh•soh•trohs, trahs] *pron pl (after prep)*
Esta carta es para **vosotros**.
Lo hago por **vosotros**.

Leisure

Food

apple *n*	**la manzana**
	[lah mahn•thah•nah] *n*
*I don't like those **apples**.*	*Estas **manzanas** no me gustan.*
banana *n*	**el plátano** [ehl plah•tah•noh] *n*
*If you want some fruit, there are **bananas** left.*	*Si quieres fruta, aún quedan **plátanos**.*
bread *n*	**el pan** [ehl pahn] *n*
*I'm going to buy some **bread**.*	*Voy a comprar **pan**.*
butter *n*	**la mantequilla**
	[lah mahn•teh•kee•yah] *n*
*Don't forget the **butter**.*	*No olvides **la mantequilla**.*

carrot n

I bought a pound of **carrots** at the market.

la zanahoria
[lah thah·nah·oh·reeyah] n
He comprado una libra de **zanahorias** en el mercado.

chicken n
I'll have the **chicken** and a glass of wine.

el pollo [ehl poh·yoh] n
Yo tomo **el pollo** y un vaso de vino.

cheese n
We have a very good **cheese**.

el queso [ehl keh·soh] n
Tenemos un **queso** buenísimo.

chocolate n

I only eat **chocolate** at the weekend.

el chocolate
[ehl choh·koh·lah·teh] n
Solo como **chocolate** los fines de semana.

fruit n
There's **fruit** for dessert.

la fruta [lah froo·tah] n
De postre hay **fruta**.

garlic n
Garlic is very good for your health.

el ajo [ehl ah·khoh] n
El ajo es muy bueno para la salud.

grape n
This year we have so many **grapes** that we could make wine.

la uva [lah oo·bah] n
Este año tenemos tantas **uvas** que podemos hacer vino.

hake n
I'll have the **hake** and a salad.

la merluza [lah mehr·loo·zah] n
Yo tomo **la merluza** y una ensalada.

ham n
I like this **ham** very much.

el jamón [ehl khah·mohn] n
Me gusta mucho este **jamón**.

ice cream n

el helado [ehl eh·lah·doh] n

Would you like a strawberry **ice-cream**?	*¿Quieres un **helado** de fresa?*
potato n *Today there is chicken with **potatoes**.*	**la patata** [lah pah·tah·tah] n *Hoy hay pollo con **patatas**.*
prawn n *I don't like **prawns**.*	**la gamba** [lah gahm·bah] n *No me gustan **las gambas**.*
fish n *I prefer **fish** to meat.*	**el pescado** [ehl pehs·kah·doh] n *Me gusta más **el pescado** que la carne.*
lemon n *I don't have any **lemons** left.*	**el limón (pl los limones)** [ehl lee·mohn] n *No me quedan **limones**.*
meat n *I don't eat much **meat**.*	**la carne** [la kahr·neh] n *Yo no como mucha **carne**.*
oil n *The **oil** is in the kitchen.*	**el aceite** [ehl ah·theyee·teh] n ***El aceite** está en la cocina.*
olive n *Do you like **olives**?*	**la aceituna** [lah ah·theyee·too·nah] n *¿Te gustan **las aceitunas**?*

Fact

Depending on whether you are in Spain or in South America, a **tortilla** refers to two different dishes: in Spain a **tortilla** or a **tortilla española** is a potato omelette. In South Amercia, a **tortilla** is a sort of a round flat cake made with maize or wheat.

omelet *n*
For dinner there's **omelet** and a salad.

la tortilla [lah tohr·tee·yah] *n*
Para cenar hay **tortilla** y una ensalada.

orange *n*
Give me an **orange**, please.

la naranja [lah nah·rahn·khah] *n*
Dame una **naranja**, por favor.

peach *n*

I've bought a kilo of **peaches**.

el melocotón
(pl los melocotones)
[ehl meh·loh·koh·tohn] *n*
He comprado un kilo de **melocotones**.

pear *n*
We have **pears**, apples and lemons.

la pera [lah peh·rah] *n*
Tenemos **peras**, manzanas y limones.

pepper *n*

We need to add salt and **pepper**.

la pimienta
[lah pee·meeyehn·tah] *n*
Hay que añadir sal y **pimienta**.

rice *n*

The dish of the day is **rice** with chicken.

el arroz (pl los arroces)
[ehl ah·rrohth] *n*
El plato del día es **arroz** con pollo.

salad *n*

Would you like a **salad**?

la ensalada
[lah ehn·sah·lah·dah] *n*
¿Quiere usted una **ensalada**?

salt *n*
Can you pass me the **salt** please?

la sal [lah sahl] *n*
¿Me da **la sal**, por favor?

sandwich *n*

el bocadillo
[ehl boh·kah·dee·yoh] *n*

*Would you like a ham **sandwich**?* *¿Quieres un **bocadillo** de jamón?*

---

sardine *n*
*I like **sardines** very much.*

la sardina [lah sahr•dee•nah] *n*
*Me gustan mucho **las sardinas**.*

---

soup *n*
*There's a bit of **soup** left.*

la sopa [lah soh•pah] *n*
*Queda un poco de **sopa**.*

---

strawberry *n*
*There are lots of **strawberries** in this area.*

la fresa [lah freh•sah] *n*
*En esta región hay muchas **fresas**.*

---

sugar *n*
*I take my coffee with a lot of **sugar**.*

el azúcar [ehl ah•thoo•kahr] *n*
*Tomo el café con mucho **azúcar**.*

---

sweet *adj*
*Those peaches are very **sweet**.*

dulce [dool•theh] *adj*
*Estos melocotones estan muy **dulces**.*

---

the omelets

las tortillas [tohr•tee•yahs]

---

the *art*

lo [loh] *art*

---

tomato *n*
*I need a kilo of **tomatoes** for this dish.*

el tomate [ehl toh•mah•teh] *n*
*Para este plato necesito un kilo de **tomates**.*

---

tuna *n*

*We had a delicious **tuna** today.*

el atún (pl los atunes)
[ehl ah•toon] *n*
*Hoy hemos comido un **atún** riquísimo.*

---

vegetables *n*
*I bought the **vegetables** at the market.*

la verdura [lah behr•doo•rah] *n*
*He comprado **la verdura** en el mercado.*

---

vinegar n
The salad doesn't have any **vinegar**.

el vinagre [ehl bee·nah·greh] n
La ensalada no tiene **vinagre**.

Drinks

beer n
Would you like a **beer**?

la cerveza [lah thehr·beh·thah] n
¿Quieres una **cerveza**?

bottle n
Open the **bottle**.

la botella [lah boh·teh·yah] n
Abre **la botella**.

coffee n
A **coffee**, please.

el café [ehl kah·feh] n
Un **café**, por favor.

dry adj
I prefer **dry** wine.

seco, -a [seh·koh, kah] adj
Me gusta más un vino **seco**.

hot chocolate n

In this café they make a very good **hot chocolate**.

el chocolate
[ehl choh·koh·lah·teh] n
En este café hacen un **chocolate** muy bueno.

juice n
An orange **juice**, please.

el zumo [ehl thoo·moh] n
Un **zumo** de naranja, por favor.

milk n
A glass of **milk**, please.

la leche [la leh·che] n
Un vaso de **leche**, por favor.

mineral water n

Don't forget the **mineral water**!

el agua mineral
[ehl ah·gwah mee·neh·rahl] n
¡No olvides **el agua mineral**!

red wine *n*	**el vino tinto** [ehl bee•noh teen•toh] *n*
*Would you like **red wine** or white wine?*	*¿Quiere **vino tinto** o blanco?*
tea *n*	**el té** [ehl teh] *n*
*I prefer **tea** to coffee.*	*Me gusta más **el té** que el café.*
wine *n*	**el vino** [ehl bee•noh] *n*
*Do you like this **wine**?*	*¿Os gusta este **vino**?*
white wine *n*	**el vino blanco** [ehl bee•noh blahn•koh] *n*
*This **white wine** is very dry.*	*Este **vino blanco** es muy seco.*

Eating In & Out

a lot *adv*	**mucho** ['mutSo] *adv*
*I like it **a lot**.*	*Me gusta **mucho**.*
bill *n*	**la cuenta** [lah kwehn•tah] *n*
*The **bill**, please.*	***La cuenta**, por favor.*
breakfast *n*	**el desayuno** [ehl deh•sah•yoo•noh] *n*
*I've already prepared **breakfast** for you.*	*Ya os he preparado **el desayuno**.*
to have breakfast *locution*	**desayunar** [deh•sah•yoo•nahr] *v*
*What time would you like to **have breakfast**?*	*¿A qué hora quieres **desayunar**?*
to cook *v*	**cocinar** [koh•thee•nahr] *v*
*My husband **cooks** very well.*	*Mi marido **cocina** muy bien.*

cuisine *n*
We like Spanish **cuisine** very much.

la cocina [la ko·thee·nah] *n*
Nos gusta mucho **la cocina** española.

cup *n*
Where are the **cups**?

la taza [lah tah·thah] *n*
¿Dónde están **las tazas**?

dish *n*
We'll have the **dish** of the day.
The **dishes** are already on the table.

el plato [ehl plah·toh] *n*
Tomamos **el plato** del día.
Los platos ya están en la mesa.

dessert *n*
What **dessert** will you have?

el postre [ehl pohs·treh] *n*
¿Qué **postre** vas a tomar?

dinner *n*
Are you coming to **dinner** too?

la cena [lah theh·nah] *n*
¿Vienes tú también a **la cena**?

to have dinner *locution*
We'd like to have **dinner** at nine.

cenar [theh·nahr] *v*
Queremos **cenar** a las nueve.

to drink *v*
I **drink** a lot of water.

beber [beh·behr] *v*
Bebo mucha agua.

to eat *v*
I don't want to **eat** yet.

comer [koh·mehr] *v*
No quiero **comer** todavía.

Food/meal *n*
There's a bit of **food** left the fridge.
You shouldn't skip **meals**.
We'll see each other at **meal** time.

la comida [lah koh·mee·dah] *n*
Queda un poco de **comida** en la nevera.
No hay que saltarse **las comidas.**
Nos vemos a la hora de **la comida.**

fork *n*
I'm looking for the **forks**.

el tenedor [ehl teh·neh·dohr] *n*
Estoy buscando los **tenedores**.

Fact

The short form **buen** is used instead of the form **bueno** before masculine singular nouns. If the adjective is placed after the noun, then the longer form **bueno** is used.

glass *n*
Would you like a **glass** of hot milk?

el vaso [ehl bah·soh] *n*
¿Quieres un **vaso** de leche caliente?

good *adj*
This wine is very **good**.

bueno, -a [bweh·noh, nah] *adj*
Este vino es muy **bueno**.

gram *n*
Give me two hundred **grams** of chorizo, please.

el gramo [ehl grah·moh] *n*
Póngame doscientos **gramos** de chorizo, por favor.

to have (food/drink) *v*
Would you like something?

tomar [toh·mahr] *v*
¿Quiere **tomar** algo?

here *adv*
There's nobody **here**.
Our friends would like to come **here**.

aquí [ah·kee] *adv*
Aquí no hay nadie.
Nuestros amigos quieren venir **aquí**.

Fact

Feminine nouns starting with a stressed **a**- or **ha**- (e.g. **hambre**) always use the masculine definite article el and the singular indefinite article as this makes them easier to pronounce. The agreement for adjectives will always be feminine though, e.g. **el agua fría** or in the sample above '**mucha hambre**'.

hot *adj*
The soup is very **hot**.

caliente [kah·leeyehn·teh] *adj*
La sopa está muy **caliente**.

hunger *n*
to be hungry *locution*

el hambre [ehl ahm·breh] *n*
tener hambre [teh·ner ahm·breh]

I'm really **hungry**.

Tengo mucha **hambre**.

like *v*
Would you **like** a beer?

querer [keh·rehr] *v*
¿**Quieres** una cerveza?

liter *n*
I drink two **liters** of water per day.

el litro [ehl lee·troh] *n*
Bebo dos **litros** de agua al día.

kilo *n*
A **kilo** costs five euros.

el quilo [ehl kee·loh] *n*
El quilo cuesta cinco euros.

kilogram *n*

el quilogramo
[ehl kee·loh·grah·moh] *n*

Give me a **kilogram** of
apples, please.

Dame un **quilogramo** de
manzanas, por favor.

knife *n*
There are no **knives**.

el cuchillo [ehl koo·chee·yoh] *n*
Faltan los **cuchillos**.

to like *v*
Did you **like** the soup?

gustar [goos·tahr] *v*
¿Os ha **gustado** la sopa?

me *pron*

mí [mee] *pron m/f*
(after preposition)

What did he say about **me**?
I like this wine a lot.

¿Qué ha dicho sobre **mí**?
A **mí** me gusta mucho este vino.

menu *n*
Waiter, could I have the
menu, please?

la carta [lah kahr·tah] *n*
Camarero, **la carta**, por favour.

menu *n*
The **menu** of the day costs fifteen euros.

el menú [ehl meh·noo] *n*
El menú del día cuesta quince euros.

. . . .

to to be missing *locution*
There's a glass **missing** here.

faltar [fahl·tahr] *v*
Aquí **falta** un vaso.

> ### Fact
>
> **Más** can be used before an adjective to form the comparative or the superlative. The superlative is formed with the construction **el más** + adjective, **la más** + adjective or **lo más** + adjective.

more *adv*
I like this **more**.
I need **more** money.

más [mahs] *adv*
Esto me gusta **más**.
Necesito **más** dinero.

. . . .

or *conj*
Would you like coffee **or** tea?

o [oh] *conj*
¿Quieres café **o** té?

. . . .

to order *v*
Are you ready **to order** yet?

pedir [peh·deer] *v*
¿Quiere **pedir** ya?

. . . .

other, another *pron*
Another coffee, please.

otro, -a [oh·troh, trah] *pron*
Otro café, por favor.

. . . .

piece *n*
Try this **piece** of bread.

el trozo [ehl troh·thoh] *n*
Prueba este **trozo** de pan.

. . . .

restaurant *n*

There's a new **restaurant** in the center.

el restaurante
[ehl rehs·taw·rahn·teh] *n*
Hay un **restaurante** nuevo en el centro.

. . . .

spoon n   **la cuchara** [lah koo•chah•rah] n
Can you pass me a **spoon**, please? ¿Me das una **cuchara**, por favor?

to be taken locution   **ocupado, -a**
     [oh•koo•pah•doh, dah] adj
This **table is taken**.   Esta mesa está **ocupada**.

something pron n   **algo** [ahl•goh] pron n
Would you like **something**   ¿Quieres **algo** de beber?
to drink?

there adv   **allí** [ah•yee] adv
There's a free table over **there**.   **Allí** hay una mesa libre.

thirst n   **la sed** [lah sehth] n
thirsty adj
to be thirsty locution
I'm very **thirsty**.   Tengo mucha **sed**.

toilets / restrooms n   **los servicios**
     [lohs sehr•bee•thee•ohs] n pl
The **toilets** are here on the right.   **Los servicios** están allí a la derecha.

gentlemen n   **caballeros** [kah•bah•yeh•rohs]
     n m pl
Where is the **men's** toilet?   Dónde están los **caballeros**?

to try v   **probar** [proh•bahr] v
I'd like **to try** this wine.   Quiero **probar** este vino.

waiter n   **el camarero**
     [ehl kah•mah•reh•roh] n
The **waiter** is coming right away. **El camarero** viene enseguida.
Waiter, could I have the bill, please? **Camarero,** la cuenta, por favor.

waitress *n*	**la camarera**
	[lah kah·mah·reh·rah] *n*
*I'll call the **waitress**.*	*Voy a llamar a **la camarera**.*

what *pron*	**qué** [keh] *pron*
***What** will you have?*	*¿**Qué** toma usted?*
*I don't know **what** to do.*	*No sé **qué** hacer.*

| **without** *prep* | **sin** [seen] *prep* |
| *It's a house **without** a garden.* | *Es una casa **sin** jardín.* |

| **you** *pron sing (polite form)* | **usted** [oos·tehd] *pron m/f sing (after prep)* |
| *We've saved a table for **you**.* | *Hemos reservado una mesa para **usted**.* |

Sports & Social

| **ball** *n* | **la pelota** [lah peh·loh·tah] *n* |
| *I found a **ball** in the street.* | *He encontrado una **pelota** en la calle.* |

| **bar** *n* | **el bar** [ehl bahr] *n* |
| *The **bar** where we have breakfast is 200 meters from here.* | ***El bar** dónde tomamos desayuno está a doscientos metros de aquí.* |

| **before** *prep* | **antes de** [ahn·tehs deh] *prep* |
| *You should eat something **before** going to the cinema.* | ***Antes de** ir al cine tienes que comer algo.* |

bicycle *n*	**la bicicleta**
	[lah bee·thee·kleh·tah] *n*
*Do you know how to ride a **bicycle**?*	*¿Sabes montar en **bicicleta**?*

| **book** *n* | **el libro** [ehl lee·broh] *n* |
| *I bought two **books** yesterday.* | *Ayer compré dos **libros**.* |

cafe n
*We sat in the terrace of the **cafe**.*

el café [ehl kah·feh] n
*Nos sentamos en la terraza de un **café**.*

---

cafe n

*We can get something to eat in the **café**.*

la cafetería
[lah kah·feh·teh·reeah] n
*Podemos comer algo en **la cafetería**.*

CD n

*I have a new **CD**.*

el disco compacto
[ehl dees·koh kohm·pahk·toh] n
*Tengo un nuevo **disco compacto**.*

---

cinema n
*Shall we go to the **cinema** or the theatre?*

el cine [el 'Tine] n
*¿Y si vamos al **cine** o al teatro?*

---

concert n

*On Sundays there are **concerts** in the square.*

el concierto
[ehl kohn·thee·ehr·toh] n
*Los domingos hay **conciertos** en la plaza.*

---

to dance v
*On saturdays we go out **dancing**.*

bailar [bahee·lahr] v
*Los sábados solemos ir a **bailar**.*

---

exhibition n

*Have you already seen the **exhibition**?*

la exposición
[lah ehx·poh·see·theeyohn] n
(pl las exposiciones)
*¿Has visitado ya **la exposición**?*

---

to fish v
*We went to the lake to **fish**.*

pescar [pehs·kahr] v
*Fuimos al lago a **pescar**.*

---

football n
*I like f**ootball** a lot.*

el fútbol [ehl foot·bohl] n
*A mí me gusta mucho **el fútbol**.*

free *adj*
Wednesday is my day **off**.
I am not **free** Wednesday night.

libre [lee•breh] *adj*
El miércoles es mi día **libre**.
Los miércoles por la noche no estoy **libre**.

---

to go for

Do you want **to go for** a coffee?

ir a tomar algo
[eer ah toh•mahr ahl•goh] *locution*
¿Quieres **ir a tomar** un café?

---

to go out *v*
Eva has **gone out** with her friends.

salir [sah•leer] *v*
Eva ha **salido** con sus amigos.

---

it *pron*
We saw **it** (the film) at cinema, Mrs Lemos.

la [lah] *pron f*
La hemos visto en el cine, señora Lemos. (la película)

---

music *n*
I don't like this **music** very much.

la música [lah moo•see•kah] *n*
Esta **música** no me gusta mucho.

---

to play *v*
Do you know how **to play** the guitar?

tocar [toh•kahr] *v*
¿Sabes **tocar** la guitarra?

Fact

When **tocar** is used to mean 'play a musical instrument', the name of the musical instrument is always preceded by a definite article (**el, la, los, las**). To play a sport, see page 106.

---

to meet *v*

We're going **to meet** Marta at five o'clock.

encontrarse
[ehn•kohn•trahr•seh] *v pr*
A las cinco nos **encontramos** con Marta.

to play *v*
The children have stopped **playing**.

jugar [khoo•gahr] *v*
Los niños han dejado de **jugar**.

to play a sport *v*
We **played** tennis.

jugar a [khu•gahr ah] *v* + *def art*
Hemos **jugado** al tenis.

Fact

When talking about playing sports or games, we use the construction **jugar a** + definite article. For musical instruments, see page 105.

---

to read *v*
I like **reading** this book.

leer [leh•ehr] *v*
Quiero **leer** este libro.

to have a rest *v*
I need **to rest** a little.

descansar [dehs•kahn•sahr] *v*
Tengo que **descansar** un poco.

to sing *v*
Pepe **sings** and plays the guitar.

cantar [kahn•tahr] *v*
Pepe **canta** y toca la guitarra.

sport *n*
Football is a **sport** that I like very much.

el deporte [ehl deh•pohr•teh] *n*
El fútbol es un **deporte** que me gusta mucho.

to play sport *v*

Do you play much **sport**?

practicar deporte
[prahk•tee•kahr deh•pohr•teh]
locution
¿**Practicas** mucho deporte?

to go for a stroll *v*

On Sunday we would like **to go for a stroll**.

dar un paseo
[dahr oon pah•seh•oh] *v*
El domingo queremos ir a **dar un paseo**.

to swim v
You need to learn how to **swim**.

nadar [nah·dahr] v
Deberías aprender a **nadar**.

to go for a swim v
I went for **a swim** in the sea.

bañarse [bah·nyahr·seh] v pr
Me he **bañado** en el mar.

swimming pool n
There is nobody in the **swimming pool** today.

la piscina [lah pees·thee·nah] n
Hoy no hay nadie bañándose en **la piscina**.

tennis n
I really like playing **tennis**.

el tenis [ehl teh·nees] n
Me gusta mucho jugar al **tenis**.

theatre n
The **theatre** is closed in the summer.

el teatro [ehl teh·ah·troh] n
El teatro está cerrado en verano.

us pron

Are you coming with **us** to the cinema?

nosotros, -as [noh·soh·trohs, trahs] pron pl (after prep)
¿Vienes con **nosotros** al cine?

walk n
We will do a big **walk**.

el paseo [ehl pah·seh·oh] n
Hicimos un largo **paseo**.

you pron pl
We saw **you** in the park.
We've sent **you** a letter.

os [ohs] pron m/f pl
Os hemos visto en el parque.
Os hemos mandado una carta.

Shopping

bag n
Can you give me a **bag** for the bread?

la bolsa [lah bohl·sah] n
¿Me puedes dar una **bolsa** para el pan?

bakery n	**la panadería**
	[lah pah•nah•deh•reeyah] n
The **bakery** is already closed.	**La panadería** ya está cerrada.
but conj	**pero** [peh•roh] conj
This oil is expensive, **but** good.	Este aceite es caro, **pero** bueno.
butcher's (shop) n .	**la carnicería**
	[lah kahr•nee•theh•reeyah] n
Excuse me, is there a **butcher's** near here?	Perdón, ¿sabe usted si hay una **carnicería** por aquí?

Fact

The adjective **barato** used in a phrase with the verb **ser** means that the item we are talking about is generally cheap (see entry for cheap); if it is used with the verb **estar** however, it means that the item in question is normally expensive, but unusually cheap in that instance.

to change v	**cambiar** [kahm•beeyahr] v
If it doesn't suit me, can I **change** it?	Si no me queda bien, ¿lo podré **cambiar**?
cheap adj	**barato, -a** [bah•rah•toh, tah] adj
These books are very **cheap.**	Estos libros son muy **baratos**.
to decide v	**decidirse** [deh•thee•deer•seh] v pr
My friend has still not **decided**.	Mi amiga todavía no se ha **decidido**.
expensive adj	**caro, -a** [kah•roh, rah] adj
Those glasses are very **expensive**.	Estas gafas son muy **caras**.
to close v	**cerrar** [theh•rraahr] v
The shops **close** at eight.	Las tiendas **cierran** a las ocho.

to buy v
I'm going **to buy** something to eat.

comprar [kohm·prahr] v
Voy a **comprar** algo para comer.

to cost v
How much do those glasses **cost**?

costar [kohs·tahr] v
¿Cuanto **cuestan** estas gafas?

euro n
This sweater costs fifty **euros**.

el euro [ew·roh] n
Este jersey cuesta cincuenta **euros**.

to go v
I'm **going** to the shop.

ir a [eer ah] v aux + inf
Voy a **ir al** supermercado.

greengrocer's / fruit shop n
The **greengrocer's** opens at nine.

la frutería [lah froo·teh·reeyah] n
La **frutería** abre a las nueve.

hairdresser's n

la peluquería
[lah peh·loo·keh·reeyah] n

I'm looking for a **hairdresser's**.

Estoy buscando una **peluquería**.

market n
They also sell flowers at
the **market**.

el mercado [ehl mehr·kah·doh] n
En **el mercado** también venden
flores.

to open v
What time do the shops **open**?

abrir [ah·breer] v
¿A qué hora **abren** las tiendas?

other adj

el otro, la otra
[ehl oh·troh, lah oh·trah] pron

I like this one more than the
other one.

Este me gusta más que **el otro**.

to pay v
Today I am **paying**.

pagar [pah·gahr] v
Hoy **pago** yo.

price n
Have you seen the **price** of this car?

el precio [ehl preh·theeyoh] n
¿Has visto **el precio** de este coche?

round here *locution*
There are lots of shops
round here.

por aquí [pohr ah·kee] *locution*
Por aquí hay muchas tiendas.

shop *n*
There are lots of **shops** on
the streets.

la tienda [lah teeyehn·dah] *n*
En esta calle hay muchas **tiendas**.

to sell *v*
I'm going **to sell** my car.

vender [behn·dehr] *v*
Voy a **vender** mi coche.

supermarket *n*

The **supermarket** closes at one.

el supermercado
[ehl soo·pehr·mehr·kah·doh] *n*
El supermercado cierra a la una.

this/these *pron*

This car is very expensive.
I like **this** house very much.

este, esta (pl estos, estas)
[ehs·teh, ehs·tah] *pron*
Este coche es carísimo.
Esta casa me gusta mucho.

those *pron*

I like **those** shoes very much.

ese, esa (pl esos, esas)
[eh·seh, sah] *pron*
Esos zapatos me gustan mucho.

till *n*
Could you pay at the **till**, please.

la caja [lah kah·khah] *n*
Pague usted en **la caja**, por favor.

together *adv*
I'm paying for everything **together**.

junto [khoon·toh] *adv*
Pago todo **junto**.

yes *adv*
Do you like it? - **Yes**.

sí [see] *adv*
¿Te gusta? – **Sí**.

yet *adv*

It's not open **yet**.

todavía no
[toh·dah·bee·ah noh] *adv*
Todavía no está abierto.

Essentials

Weather & Climate

air *n*
*I like the mountain **air**.*

el aire [ehl ahee·reh] *n*
*Me gusta **el aire** de la montaña.*

hot *adj*
*Come and swim, the water
is **hot**!*

caliente [kah·leeyehn·teh] *adj*
*¡Ven a bañarte, el agua está
caliente!*

to be hot *locution*

*It was very **hot** yesterday.*
*It's **hot** today.*

hacer calor
[ah·thehr kah·lohr] *locution*
*Ayer hizo mucho **calor**.*
***Hace calor** hoy.*

to change *v*
*The weather has **changed**.*

cambiar [kahm·beeyahr] *v*
*El tiempo ha **cambiado**.*

cold *n*
*Why do you like the **cold** so much?*

el frío [ehl free·oh] *n*
*¿Por qué os gusta tanto **el frío**?*

cold adj	**frío, -a** [free•oh, ah] adj
The water is so **cold**!	¡Qué **fría** está el agua!
to be cold locution	**hacer frío** [ah•thehr free•oh] locution
Today it's very **cold**.	Hoy hace mucho **frío**.

Fact

Hacer frío and **tener frío** express different things. **Hacer frío** is used when referring to the cold in a general context ('it is cold' when talking about the weather), whereas **tener frío** is used to express the sensation, i.e. feeling cold.

to rain v	**llover** [yoh•behr] v
We can't go out, it's **raining**.	No podemos salir, está **lloviendo**.
sun n	**el sol** [ehl sohl] n
I don't like the **sun** very much.	No me gusta mucho **el sol**.
to be sunny locution	**hacer sol** [ah•thehr sohl] locution
It's **sunny** today.	Hoy **hace sol**.
shade n	**la sombra** [lah sohm•brah] n
It's cold in the **shade**.	En **la sombra** hace frío.
very adv	**muy** [mooy] adv
The water is **very** cold.	El agua está **muy** fría.
You speak Spanish **very** well.	Hablas **muy** bien español.
water n	**el agua** [ehl ah•gwah] n
The price of **water** has gone up a lot.	El precio del **agua** ha subido mucho.

weather *n*	**el tiempo** [ehl teeyehm·poh] *n*
I don't like this **weather**.	No me gusta este **tiempo**.
bad weather *locution*	**hacer mal tiempo** [ah·thehr mahl teeyehm·poh] *locution*
When the **weather** is bad, I don't like going out.	Cuando **hace mal tiempo** no me gusta salir.
good weather *locution*	**hacer buen tiempo** [ah·thehr booehn teeyehm·poh] *locution*
Today the **weather** is very **good**.	Hoy hace muy **buen tiempo**.
with *prep*	**con** [kohn] *prep*
We cannot go out **in** this weather.	**Con** este tiempo no se puede salir.

Fact

The short form **mal** is used instead of the form **malo** before masculine singular nouns. If the adjective is placed after the noun, then the longer form **malo** is used.

Holidays & Travel

after *prep*	**después de** [dehs·pwehs deh] *prep*
After the cinema we'll go and have something to drink.	**Después** del cine vamos a tomar algo.
beach *n*	**la playa** [lah plah·yah] *n*
The **beach** is two kilometers away.	**La playa** está a dos kilómetros.

bridge *n*	**el puente** [ehl poo•ehn•teh] *n*
This **bridge** is new.	Este **puente** es nuevo.
campsite *n*	**el camping (pl los campings)** [ehl kahm•peeng] *n*
The **campsite** is full.	**El camping** está completo.
capital *n*	**la capital** [lah kah•pee•tahl] *n*
Do you know what the **capital** is called?	¿Sabes cómo se llama **la capital**?
castle *n*	**el castillo** [ehl kahs•tee•yoh] *n*
This **castle** is very old.	Este **castillo** es muy antiguo.
church *n*	**la iglesia** [lah ee•gleh•seeyah] *n*
The **church** is closed.	**La iglesia** está cerrada.
city *n* **town** *n*	**la ciudad** [lah theeyoo•dahd] *n*
Do you know the **city** already?	¿Ya conocéis **la ciudad**?
double room *n*	**la habitación doble** [lah ah•bee•tah•theeyohn doh•bleh] *n*
We need two **double rooms**.	Necesitamos dos **habitaciones dobles**.
entrance *n*	**la entrada** [lah ehn•trah•dah] *n*
This is the front **entrance**.	Esta es la puerta de **entrada**.
exit *n*	**la salida** [lah sah•lee•dah] *n*
We're looking for the **exit**.	Estamos buscando **la salida**.
for *prep*	**por** [pohr] *prep*
I bought this suitcase **for** fifty euros.	He comprado esta maleta **por** cincuenta euros.

It's **for** my sister.	Es **por** mi hermana.
I sometimes come around here.	Vengo a menudo **por** aquí.
from *prep*	**desde** [dehs·deh] *prep*
You can call **from** here.	**Desde** aquí podéis llamar.
full *adj*	**completo, -a** [kohm·pleh·toh,tah] *adj*
The hotel is **full**.	El hotel está **completo**.
full board *n*	**la pensión completa** [lah pehn·see·ohn kohm·pleh·tah] *n*
We have a hotel with **full board**.	Tenemos un hotel con **pensión completa**.
to go *v*	**ir** [eer] *v*
I'm **going** to the museum.	**Voy** al museo.
half board *n*	**la media pensión** [lah meh·deeah pehn·see·ohn] *n*
We paid eighty euros for **half board**.	Hemos pagado ochenta euros por **la media pensión**.
holidays *n*	**las vacaciones** [lahs bah·kah·thee·oh·nehs] *n*
They have already started their **holidays**.	Ya han empezado **las vacaciones**.
Last year we **holidayed** in France.	El año pasado estuvimos de **vacaciones** en Francia.
to go on holidays *v*	**ir de vacaciones** [eer deh bah·kah·thee·oh·nehs] *locution*
My parents always **go on holidays** to Italy.	Mis padres siempre van **de vacaciones** a Italia.

hotel *n*	**el hotel** [ehl oh·tehl] *n*
I reserved a **hotel**.	He reservado **el hotel**.
in *prep*	**en** [en] *prep*
Nobody comes **in** winter.	**En** invierno no viene nadie.
Island *n*	**la isla** [lah ees·lah] *n*
We always go to an **island** on holidays.	En las vacaciones siempre vamos a alguna **isla**.
long *adj*	**largo, -a** [lahr·goh, gah] *adj*
We're going on a very **long** trip.	Vamos a hacer un viaje muy **largo**.
a long time *locution*	**mucho tiempo** [moo·choh teeyehm·poh] *adv*
Will you stay a **long time**?	¿Va a quedarse usted **mucho tiempo**?
map *n*	**el mapa** [ehl mah·pah] *n*
Do you have a **map** of this region?	¿Tiene un **mapa** de esta región?
museum *n*	**el museo** [ehl moo·seh·oh] *n*
The **museum** is in the centre of town.	**El museo** está en el centro de la ciudad.
to pack your bags	**hacer la maleta** [ah·thehr lah mah·leh·tah] *locution*
Patricia, have you **packed your bags**?	Patricia, ¿**has hecho** ya tu **maleta**?
park *n*	**el parque** [ehl pahr·keh] *n*
We met in the **park**.	Nos hemos encontrado en **el parque**.
photo *n*	**la foto** [lah foh·toh] *n*

Do you want to see the **photos** of our trip to Spain?	¿Quieres ver **las fotos** de nuestro viaje a España?
port n The bus goes to the **port**.	**el puerto** [ehl poo·ehr·toh] n El autobús va hasta **el puerto**.
postcard n	**la tarjeta postal** [lah tahr·kheh·tah pohs·tahl] n, abbr postal
I am going to send him a **postcard** from Valencia.	Le voy a mandar una **tarjeta postal** desde Valencia.
pretty adj How **pretty** is this beach!	**bonito, -a** [boh·nee·toh,tah] adj ¡Qué **bonita** es esta playa!
to reserve v Would you like **to reserve** a table?	**reservar** [reh·sehr·bahr] v ¿Queréis que **reserve** una mesa?
short adj This year we're going on a **short** trip.	**corto, -a** [kohr·toh, tah] adj Este año vamos a hacer un viaje **corto**.
single room n	**la habitación individual** [lah ah·bee·tah·theeyohn een·dee·bee·doo·ahl] n
A **single room** costs sixty euros.	**La habitación individual** cuesta sesenta euros.
some pron There are **some** houses here that I really like.	**unos, -as** [oo·nohs, nahs] art Aquí hay **unas** casas que me gustan mucho.
square n In the centre there's a large **square**.	**la plaza** [lah plah·thah] n En el centro hay una **plaza** grande.

suitcase / bag *n* Where is my **suitcase**?	**la maleta** [lah mah•leh•tah] *n* ¿Dónde está mi **maleta**?
to sunbathe We **sunbathed** on the beach.	**tomar el sol** [toh•mahr ehl sohl] *locution* Hemos **tomado el sol** en la playa.
tourist information office *n* Let's ask in the **tourist information office**.	**la oficina de turismo** [lah oh•fee•thee•nah deh too•rees•moh] *n* **Preguntemos en la oficina de turismo.**
to travel *v* My parents **travel** a lot.	**viajar** [beeah•khahr] *v* Mis padres **viajan** mucho.
trip *n* This year we're going to do a big **trip**.	**el viaje** [ehl beeah•kheh] *n* Este año vamos a hacer un largo **viaje.**
typical *adj* It's a **typical** dish in this region.	**típico, -a** [tee•pee•koh] *adj* Es un plato **típico** de esta región.
you *pron sg* I saw **you** at the cinema. Do **you** like this wine?	**te** [teh] *pron m/f* **Te** he visto en el cine. ¿**Te** gusta este vino?
you *pron sg* This present is for **you**. We talked about **you**.	**ti** [tee] *pron m/f (after prep)* Este regalo es para **ti**. Hemos hablado de **ti**.
to visit *v* Today we **visited** a really interesting museum.	**visitar** [bee•see•tahr] *v* Hoy hemos **visitado** un museo interesantísimo.

you *pron pl*
We saw **you** in the park.
We've sent **you** a letter.

os [ohs] *pron m/f pl*
Os hemos visto en el parque.
Os hemos mandado una carta.

Days of the Week

Monday *n*
We'll see each other on **Monday**.

el lunes [ehl loo•nehs] *n*
Nos vemos **el lunes**.

On Mondays *adv*
On Mondays I get up at six.

los lunes [lohs loo•nehs] *adv*
Los lunes me levanto a las seis.

Tuesday *n*
Every **Tuesday** I go to the
cinema with Ricardo.
On Tuesdays *adv*
On Tuesdays I work in
the morning.

el martes [ehl mahr•tehs] *n*
Cada **martes** voy al cine con
Ricardo.
los martes [lohs mahr•tehs] *adv*
Trabajo **los martes** por la mañana.

Wednesday *n*

Wednesday is my day off.

el miércoles
[ehl meeyehr•koh•lehs] *n*
El miércoles es mi día libre.

Fact

Notice that the days of the week are always preceded by the definite
article **el** or **los** in the plural, e.g. **los domingos**.

On Wednesdays *adv*

We don't cook **on Wednesdays**.

los miércoles
[lohs meeyehr•koh•lehs] *adv*
Los miércoles no cocinamos.

119

Thursday n *My parents are coming back on **Thursday**.*	**el jueves** [ehl khooeh•behs] n *Mis padres vuelven **el jueves**.*
on Thursdays adv *My parents don't work on **Thursdays**.*	**los jueves** [los khooeh•behs] adv *Mis padres no trabajan **los jueves**.*
Friday n *Do you have time on **Friday**?*	**el viernes** [ehl beeyehr•nehs] n *¿Tienes tiempo **el viernes**?*
on Fridays adv *I don't work **on Fridays**.*	**los viernes** [lohs beeyehr•nehs] adv *No trabajo **los viernes**.*
Saturday n *We meet Eva every **Saturday** at the market.*	**el sábado** [ehl sah•bah•doh] n *Vemos a Eva cada **sábado** en el mercado.*
on Saturdays adv *I don't like cooking **on Saturdays**.*	**los sábados** [lohs sah•bah•dohs] adv ***Los sábados** no me gusta cocinar.*
Sunday n *On **Sunday** I'll go for a walk with my mother.*	**el domingo** [ehl doh•meen•goh] n ***El domingo** voy a dar un paseo con mi madre.*
on Sundays adv	**los domingos** [lohs doh•meen•gohs] adv

I always go to the cinema on **Sundays**.	**Los domingos** voy siempre al cine.
day n	**el día** [ehl dee·ah] n
We will stay for four **days**.	Nos quedaremos cuatro **días.**
I slept all **day** long.	He dormido todo **el día**.
today adv	**hoy** [ohee] adv
Today it's closed.	**Hoy** está cerrado.
tomorrow adv	**mañana** [mah·nyah·nah] adv
Tomorrow is Tuesday.	**Mañana** es martes.
week n	**la semana** [lah seh·mah·nah] n
We're staying a **week**.	Nos vamos a quedar una **semana**.
weekend n	**el fin de semana** [ehl feen deh seh·mah·nah] n
What are you doing this **weekend**?	¿Qué haces este **fin de semana**?
yesterday adv	**ayer** [ah·yehr] adv
We went on an excursion **yesterday**.	**Ayer** hicimos una excursión.

Special Days

Ascension n	**la Ascensión** [lah ahs·thehn·seeyohn] n
Today is the Feast of the **Ascension**.	Hoy es **la Ascensión**.

All Saints Day n

el día de Todos los Santos
[ehl deeah deh toh·dohs
lohssahn·tohs] n

On **All Saint's Day** we have dinner at my mother's house.

El día de Todos los Santos comemos en casa de mi madre.

Birthday n

el cumpleaños
[ehl koom·pleh·ah·nyohs] n

Happy **Birthday!**

*¡Feliz **cumpleaños!***

Christmas n

la Navidad
[lah nah·bee·dahd] n

Happy **Christmas!**

*¡Feliz **Navidad!***

Christmas Eve n

la Nochebuena
[lah no·cheh·booeh·nah] n

On **Christmas Eve**, we go to mass.

*En **Nochebuena** vamos a la Misa del Gallo.*

We will have dinner at my sister's house on **Christmas Eve**.

*En **Nochebuena** cenamos en casa de mi hermana.*

Corpus Christi n

el día del Corpus Christi
[ehl deeah dehl kohr·poos krees·tee] n

Tomorrow is **Corpus Christi**.

*Mañana es **día del Corpus Christi**.*

Easter n

la Pascua [lah pahs·kooah] n

At **Easter** we're going to Paris.

*En **Pascua** nos vamos a París.*

Good Friday n

el Viernes Santo
[ehl bee·ehr·nehs sahn·toh] n

Good Friday is celebrated in Spain.

*El **Viernes Santo** es festivo en España.*

Fact

Fact

The plural form **las Pascuas** refers to Christmas: so the expression **¡Felices Pascuas!** Is another way of saying 'Merry Christmas!' but does not mean 'Happy Easter!'. Easter is generally not seen as a celebratory period and is a time of mourning for Christ which is marked by the parades during **Semana Santa**, see p.123.

Holy Week *n*

la Semana Santa
[lah seh•mah•nah sahn•tah] *n*

*In Spain during **Semana Santa**, there are processions in the streets. What are you doing for **Holy Week**?*

*En España, en **Semana Santa**, hay procesiones por las calles.*
*¿Qué hacéis en **Semana Santa**?*

Fact

Semana Santa, or Holy Week, is the week in the run up to Easter. It is characterized by elaborate religious processions led by members of the local Christian brotherhood dressed in white robes with conical white hoods, similar to those worn by the Inquistion and by the Ku Klux Klan. The mood is sombre and passionate as floats carrying effigies of Christ on the Cross and the Virgin Mary in mourning pass through the crowded streets. See also Easter on p.122.

New Year *n*

el Año Nuevo
[ehl ah•nyoh nooeh•boh] *n*

*Tomorrow is the Chinese **New Year**.
Happy **New Year**!*

*Mañana es **el Año Nuevo** Chino.*

*¡Feliz **Año Nuevo**!*

New Year's Eve *n*	**la Nochevieja** [lah noh•cheh•beeyeh•khah] *n*
On **New Year's Eve**, the Spanish eat twelve grapes.	En **Nochevieja**, los españoles toman las doce uvas.
Pentecost *n*	**el Pentecostés** [ehl pehn•teh•kohs•tehs] *n*
This year I'm staying at home for **Pentecost**.	Este año me quedo en casa en **Pentecostés**.

Months & Seasons

January *n* We're leaving on the fourth of **January**.	**enero** [eh•neh•roh] *n m* Nos vamos el cuatro de **enero**.
February *n* In **February** it's already not so cold.	**febrero** [feh•breh•roh] *n m* En **febrero** ya no hace tanto frío.
March *n* In **March** we're going on a trip to Portugal.	**marzo** [mahr•thoh] *n m* En **marzo** vamos a hacer un viaje a Portugal.
April *n* My brother starts work in **April**.	**abril** [ah•breel] *n m* Mi hermano empieza a trabajar en **abril**.
May *n* In **May** we always have a lot of work to do in the garden.	**mayo** [mah•yoh] *n m* En **mayo** siempre tenemos mucho trabajo en el jardín.

June *n*
In **June** we're going to the mountains for a week.

junio [khoo·neeyoh] *n m*
En **junio** nos vamos a la montaña por una semana.

July *n*
The children have holidays in **July**.

julio [khoo·leeyoh] *n m*
Los niños tienen vacaciones en **julio**.

August *n*
Do you know if Enrique is going to be in Mexico in **August**?

agosto [ah·gohs·toh] *n m*
¿Sabes si Enrique va a estar en México en **agosto**?

September *n*

septiembre
[sehp·teeyehm·breh] *n m*

In **September** the weather is still nice here.

En **septiembre** todavía hace buen tiempo aquí.

October *n*
The 12th of **October** is a holiday.

octubre [ohk·too·breh] *n m*
El 12 de **octubre** es día festivo.

November *n*

noviembre
[noh·beeyehm·breh] *n m*

In **November** it always rains a lot here.

En **noviembre** siempre llueve mucho aquí.

December *n*

diciembre
[dee·theeyehm·breh] n m

Maria writes that she will come and visit us in **December**.

María escribe que va a visitarnos en **diciembre**.

month *n*
I haven't seen Daniel for a **month**.

el mes [ehl mehs] *n*
No veo a Daniel desde hace un **mes**.

Fact

Months are always masculine and are used with the preposition **en: en enero** – in January. Notice that the days of the week are always preceded by the definite article, see p.119.

---

per month *locution*
How much do you earn
per **month**?

al mes [ahl mehs] *adv*
¿Cuánto ganas **al mes**?

---

autumn *n*

School starts in **autumn**.

el otoño
[ehl oh•toh•nyoh] *n*
El colegio empieza en **otoño**.

---

spring *n*

We're going on a trip in **spring**.

la primavera
[lah pree•mah•beh•rah] *n*
Vamos a hacer un viaje en
primavera.

---

summer *n*

It's very hot here in **summer**.

el verano
[ehl beh•rah•noh] *n*
En **verano** hace mucho calor aquí.

---

winter *n*

After **winter** comes the spring.

el invierno
[ehl een•beeyehr•noh] *n*
Después del **invierno** viene la
primavera.

---

year *n*
It's been a very good **year**.
I'm getting married next **year**.

el año [ehl anyoh] *n*
Ha sido un **año** muy bueno.
El año que viene me caso.

afternoon n (or evening)
The bank is closed in the **afternoons**.

la tarde [lah tahr·deh] n
El banco está cerrado por **la tarde**.

---

in the afternoon locution

Our flight arrives at 4:00 p.m. **in the afternoon**.

de la tarde [deh lah tahr·deh] locution
Nuestro vuelo llega a las cuatro **de la tarde**.

---

and
Yesterday afternoon I worked until a quarter **past** eight.

y [ee] conj
Ayer por la tarde trabajé hasta las ocho **y** cuarto.

---

at prep
Breakfast is **at** 7:00 a.m.

a [ah] prep
Desayuno **a** las siete.

At what time…? locution

At what time does the start?

¿A qué hora…?
[ah keh oh·rah] locution
¿A qué hora commenza la film pellicula?

Fact

In Spanish the date is written with the article **el**, e.g. **el cinco de octubre** (el + day + month), see '**October**' on p.125.

---

day and night locution

We have to work **day and night**.

día y noche
[dee·ah ee noh·cheh] locution
Tenemos que trabajar **día y noche**.

first *adv*
First we'll eat, then we'll look at the photos.

primero [pree•meh•roh] *adv*
Primero comemos, después miramos las fotos.

hour *n*
We'll eat in one **hour**.

la hora [lah oh•rah] *n*
En una **hora** vamos a comer.

half *adj*

It took us **half** an hour to get here.

medio, -a
[meh•deeyoh, deeyah] *adj*
Hemos tardado **media** hora en llegar.

half past *locution*

Today I ate at **half-past** three.

y media
[ee meh•deeyah] *locution*
Hoy he comido a las tres **y media**.

in the morning *locution*

The train leaves at eight **in the morning**.

de la mañana
[deh lah mah•nyah•nah] *locution*
El tren sale a las ocho **de la mañana**.

last night *adv*
Last night I listenend to the news on the radio.

anoche [ah•noh•cheh] *adv*
Anoche escuché la noticia por la radio.

later *adv*
then *adv*
I'll see Isabelle **later**.
We went to the restaurant, **then** we went to the disco.

después [dehs•pwehs] *adv*

A Isabel la veré **después**.
Fuimos al restaurante y **después** a la discoteca.

midday *n*

At **midday** we eat at the restaurant.

el mediodía
[ehl meh•deeyoh•dee•ah] *n*
A **mediodía** comemos en el restaurante.

morning n

*This shop is only open in the **morning**.*
*He's been sleeping all **morning**.*

la mañana
[lah mah•nyah•nah] n
Esta tienda abre solo por la mañana.
Ha estado toda la mañana durmiendo.

---

midnight n

*We leave at **midnight**.*

la medianoche
[lah meh•deeyah•noh•cheh] n
Saldremos a medianoche.

---

minute n

*We'll eat in ten **minutes**.*

el minuto
[ehl mee•noo•toh] n
En diez minutos comemos.

---

night n
*I read every **night**.*
*A room for two **nights**, please.*

la noche [lah noh•cheh] n
Leo cada noche.
Una habitación para dos noches.

---

now adv
Now I don't have time.

ahora [ah•oh•rah] adv
Ahora no tengo tiempo.

---

quarter n
*Let's meet at a **quarter** to six.*
*It will take you a **quarter** of an hour, twenty minutes.*

el cuarto [ehl kwahr•toh] n
Quedamos a las cinco menos cuarto.
Tardarás un cuarto de hora, veinte minutos.

---

second n

*This announcement lasts twenty **seconds**.*

el segundo
[ehl seh•goon•doh] n
Este anuncio dura veinte segundos.

---

since prep
*I've been here **since** Monday.*

desde [dehs•deh] prep
Estoy aquí desde el lunes.

time *n* What **time is** it?	**la hora** [lah oh•rah] *n* ¿Qué **hora** es?
time *n* I don't have **time** today.	**el tiempo** [ehl teeyehm•poh] *n* Hoy no tengo **tiempo**.
to (for time) It's already a quarter **to** six.	**menos** [meh•nohs] *adv* Ya son las seis **menos** cuarto.
when *adv* I always feel happy **when** I see you.	**cuando** [kwahn•doh] *conj* Siempre me alegro **cuando** te veo.

Numbers

zero	**cero** [theh•roh]
one	**uno, -a** [oo•noh, nah]
first	**primer(o), -a** [pree•mehr(oh, ah)]
two	**dos** [dohs]
second	**segundo, -a** [seh•goon•doh, dah]
three	**tres** [trehs]
third	**tercer(o), -a** [tehr•theh(roh, rah)]
four	**cuatro** [kooah•troh]
fourth	**cuarto, -a** [koo•ahr•toh, tah]
five	**cinco** [theen•koh]
fifth	**quinto, -a** [keen•toh, tah]
six	**seis** [seh•ees]

sixth	*sexto, -a* [sehx•toh, tah]
seven	**siete** [seeyeh•teh]
seventh	**séptimo, -a** [sehp•tee•moh, mah]
eight	**ocho** [oh•choh]
eighth	**octavo, -a** [ohk•tah•boh, bah]
nine	**nueve** [nooeh•beh]
ninth	**noveno, -a** [noh•beh•noh, nah]
ten	**diez** [deeyehth]
tenth	**décimo, -a** [deh•thee•moh, mah]
eleven	**once** [ohn•theh]
twelve	**doce** [doh•theh]
thirteen	**trece** [treh•theh]
fourteen	**catorce** [kah•tohr•theh]
fifteen	**quince** [keen•theh]
sixteen	**dieciséis** [deeyeh•thee•seh•ees]
seventeen	**diecisiete** [deeyeh•thee•seeyeh•teh]
eighteen	**dieciocho** [deeyeh•thee•oh•choh]
nineteen	**diecinueve** [deeyeh•thee•nooeh•beh]
twenty	**veinte** [behyeen•teh]

twenty-one	**veintiuno, -a** [behyeen·tee·oo·noh, nah]
twenty-two	**veintidós** [behyeen·tee·dohs]
twenty-three	**veintitrés** [behyeen·tee·trehs]
twenty-six	**veintiséis** [behyeen·tee·seh·ees]
thirty	**treinta** [trehyeen·tah]
thirty-one	**treinta y uno** [trehyeen·tah ee oo·noh]
forty	**cuarenta** [kooah·rehn·tah]
fifty	**cincuenta** [theen·kooehn·tah]
sixty	**sesenta** [seh·sehn·tah]
seventy	**setenta** [seh·tehn·tah]
eighty	**ochenta** [oh·chehn·tah]
ninety	**noventa** [noh·behn·tah]
one hundred	**cien** [theeyehn]
one hundred and one	**ciento uno, -a** [theeyehn·toh oo·noh, nah]
two hundred	**doscientos, -as** [dohs·theeyehn·tohs, tahs]

three hundred	**trescientos, -as** [trehs•theeyehn•tohs, tahs]
four hundred	**cuatrocientos, -as** [kooah•troh•theeyehn•tohs, tahs]
four hundred and thirty-seven	**cuatrocientos treinta y siete** **cuatrocientas treinta y siete** [kooah•troh•theeyehn•tohs trehyeen•tah ee seeyeh•teh, kooah•troh•theeyehn•tahs trehyeen•tah ee seeyeh•teh]
five hundred	**quinientos, -as** [kee•neeyehn•tohs, tahs]
six hundred	**seiscientos, -as** [seh•ees•theeyehn•tohs, tahs]
seven hundred	**setecientos, -as** [seh•teh•theeyehn•tohs, tahs]
eight hundred	**ochocientos, -as** [oh•choh•theeyehn•tohs, tahs]
nine hundred	**novecientos, -as** [noh•beh•theeyehn•tohs, tahs]
one thousand	**mil** [meel]
two thousand	**dos mil** [dohs meel]
one hundred thousand	**cien mil** [theeyehn meel]
one million	**un millón** [oon mee•yohn]

Quantities

all *adj*

todo, -a
[toh•doh, dah] *adj (+ art)*

*We work **all** week long.*

*Trabajamos **toda** la semana.*

as much/many

tanto ... como, tanta ... como
[tahn•to ... koh•moh, tahn•tah
...koh•moh] *adj*

*I have **as many** questions
as you have.*

*Tengo **tantas** preguntas **como** tú.*

as much as

tanto como
[tahn•toh koh•moh] *adv*

*He doesn't earn **as much as** I do.*

*No gana **tanto como** yo.*

to count *v*
*I haven't **counted** the stamps yet.*

contar [kohn•tahr] *v*
*Todavía no he **contado** los sellos.*

each *adj*
***Each** house has a small garden.*

cada [kah•dah] *adj*
***Cada** casa tiene un pequeño jardín.*

enough *adj*

suficiente
[soo•fee•theeyehn•teh] *adj*

*There isn't **enough** work
for everybody.*

*No hay trabajo **suficiente** para
todos.*

every *adj*

todos, -as
[toh•dohs, dahs] *adj (+ art)*

*Laura comes **every** day.*

*Laura viene **todos** los días.*

everyone, all *pron*

todos, -as
[toh•dohs, dahs] *n m et f*

*We're **all** going together.*

*Vamos **todos** juntos.*

everything, all *pron* That's **all**.	**todo** [ehl toh•doh] *n* Esto es **todo**.
half *adj* Could I have **half** a liter of wine, please? **Half** board is cheaper.	**medio, -a** [meh•deeyoh, deeyah] *adj* **Medio** litro de vino, por favor. La **media** pensión es más barata.
little *adj* I have **little** time.	**poco, -a** [poh•koh, kah] *adj* Tengo **poco** tiempo.
little *adv* Juan sleeps **little**.	**poco** [poh•koh] *adv* Juan duerme **poco**.
a little This wine costs **a little** more than the other one.	**un poco** [oon poh•koh] *adv* Este vino cuesta **un poco** más que el otro.
a little I drink my coffee with **a little** milk.	**un poco de** [oon poh•koh deh] *locution + n* Tomo el café con **un poco de** leche.
to have left *locution* We **have** one hour **left**. I **have** twenty euros **left**.	**quedar** [keh•dahr] *v* Nos **queda** una hora. Me **quedan** veinte euros.
more or less *locution* It's **more or less** five kilometers from here.	**más o menos** [mahs oh meh•nohs] *locution* Está a **más o menos** cien quilómetros.

much, many *adj*	**mucho, -a** [moo•choh, chah] *adj*
*There aren't **many** houses*	*En esta calle no hay **muchas** casas.*
	on this street.

| not *adv* | **no** [noh] *adv inv* |
| *I do **not** have time.* | **No** *tengo tiempo.* |

| nothing, anything *pron* | **nada** [nah•dah] *pron* |
| *I don't know **anything**.* | *Yo no sé **nada**.* |

Fact

When the negation — in this case **nada** — is placed after the verb in a phrase, the verb must also be preceded by a **no**. It is thus a double negation. See also '**nada**' on p.136.

| so *adv* | **tanto, -a** [tahn•toh, tah] *adj* |
| *I have **so** much work!* | ¡*Tengo **tanto** trabajo!* |

Asking Questions

| to agree *v* | **acordarse** [ah•kohr•dahr•seh] *v pr* |
| *I don't **agree**.* | *No **me acuerdo**.* |

| how *adv* | **cómo** [koh•moh] *pron* |
| ***How** are you?* | ¿***Cómo** está usted?* |

which *pron*	**cuál (pl cuáles)** [koo•ahl] *pron*
***Which** is the biggest city*	¿***Cuál** es la ciudad más grande del*
in the world?	*mundo?*
***Which** ones would you like?*	¿***Cuáles** quieres?*

when *adv*	**cuándo** [koo•ahn•doh] *pron*
When did you say?	*¿Cuándo se lo dijiste?*
how much *locution*	**cuánto** [koo•ahn•toh] *pron*
How much does this CD cost?	*¿Cuánto cuesta este CD?*
how many *locution*	**cuántos, -as**
	[koo•ahn•tohs, tahs] *pron pl*
How many rooms does the hotel have?	*¿Cuántas habitaciones tiene el hotel?*
that *pron*	**ese, esa (pl esos, esas)**
	[eh•seh, sah] *pron*
	eso [eh•soh] *pron n, inv*
Did you see *that*?	*¿Has visto eso?*

Fact

Eso is a demonstrative pronoun that is only used to refer to a noun. It is never used with a noun. The same rule applies to **esto**, see p.137.

What?	Qué?
What is this for?	*¿Para qué sirve eso?*
What wine do you prefer?	*¿Qué vino prefieres?*
what for *pron*	**para qué** [pah•rah keh] *pron*
What are you giving it for?	*¿Para qué lo das?*
where *pron*	**dónde** [dohn•deh] *pron*
Where do you live?	*¿Dónde vive usted?*
Where can I sit?	*¿Dónde puedo sentarme?*

Where *adv (with direction)*
Where are you going?

adónde [ah·dohn·deh] *pron*
¿Adónde va usted?

- -

where ...from *locution*
Where are you **from**?

de dónde [deh dohn·deh] *pron*
¿De dónde es usted?

- -

who *pron*
The woman **who** lives on
the second floor is Argentine.

que [kay] *pron*
La señora **que** vive en el segundo
piso es argentina.

- -

who *pron*

Who is this man?

quién (pl quiénes)
[keeyehn] *pron*
¿Quién es ese señor?

- -

whom *pron*
The Venezuelans **whom** we
met are very nice.

que [keh] *pron m/f pl*
Los venezolanos **que** hemos conocido son muy simpáticos.

- -

why *adv*
Why haven't you started yet?

por qué [pohr keh] *pron*
¿Por qué no habéis empezado
todavía?

Index

English

140

B

C

G

go to sleep 60
goat 38
good 12, 21, 83, 99
good afternoon 83
Good Friday 123
good night 83
good weather 113
goodbye 8
gram 99
grandfather 19
grandmother 19
grape 92
grass 38
Great Britain 28

green 41
greengrocer's / fruit shop 109
greet 84
grey 41
Guatemala 29
Guatemalan 29

H

hair 44
hairbrush 44
hairdresser's 109
hake 92
half 115, 128, 135
half board 115
half past 128
ham 92
hand 44
handsome 13
happy 13, 15
to have 53, 57, 99
to have a rest 106

to have breakfast 96
to have dinner 98
to have left 135
to have to 57, 84
he 29
head 44
headache 48
health 48
healthy 48
hear 13
hello 84
help 78
her 13, 71, 78
here 99, 110
hi 84
him 53, 71, 84
Himself/herself/themselves 53
his/her 13, 19
holidays 113, 115, 116
Holy Week 123
home 57, 58
Honduran 29
Honduras 29
hope 19
horse 38
hospital 48
hot 48, 61, 99, 111
hot chocolate 96
hotel 116
hour 128
house 54
how 136
how many/how much 137
hunger 100

Q

R

S

C000134186

FOR THE BEST

DAD

EVER

summersdale

FOR THE BEST DAD EVER

An Hachette UK Company
www.hachette.co.uk

Summersdale Publishers Ltd
Part of Octopus Publishing Group Limited
Carmelite House
50 Victoria Embankment
LONDON
EC4Y 0DZ
UK

www.summersdale.com

Printed and bound in China

ISBN: 978-1-78783-235-0

TO Dad

Lots of love

FROM Claire
e
Paul
x x x

FATHERING IS NOT

SOMETHING PERFECT

MEN DO, BUT SOMETHING

THAT PERFECTS THE MAN.

FRANK PITTMAN

MY DAD
BELIEVED
IN ME, EVEN
WHEN I
DIDN'T.

TAYLOR SWIFT

My dad has given me
the best gift anyone
has ever given me. He
gave me wings to fly.

ADRIA ARJONA

OTHER THINGS MAY CHANGE US, BUT WE START AND END WITH THE FAMILY.

ANTHONY BRANDT

"

I've jumped out of helicopters...
and played baseball in a
professional stadium, but none
of it means anything compared
to being somebody's daddy.

CHRIS PRATT

"

My daddy was my hero –
he was always there for
me when I needed him.

BINDI IRWIN

I FEEL BAD FOR
OTHER PEOPLE...
I CLEARLY GOT
THE BEST DAD!

MY FATHER WAS MY TEACHER. BUT MOST IMPORTANTLY HE WAS A GREAT DAD.

BEAU BRIDGES

"

You can tell what was the
best year of your father's life,
because they seem to freeze that
clothing style and ride it out.

JERRY SEINFELD

"

Never is a man more of a man than when he is the father of a newborn.

MATTHEW McCONAUGHEY

A FATHER IS A GIANT

FROM WHOSE

SHOULDERS YOU CAN

SEE FOR EVER.

PERRY GARFINKEL

Govern a family as you would cook a small fish – very gently.

CHINESE PROVERB

"

I love my father as the stars – he's a bright shining example and a happy twinkling in my heart.

TERRI GUILLEMETS

"

Dad taught me everything
I know. Unfortunately,
he didn't teach me
everything he knows.

AL UNSER JR

DAD IS JUST ANOTHER WORD FOR HOME.

BLESSED INDEED IS THE MAN WHO HEARS MANY GENTLE VOICES CALL HIM FATHER!

LYDIA M. CHILD

JUST TAUGHT MY
KIDS ABOUT TAXES BY
EATING 38 PER CENT
OF THEIR ICE CREAM.

CONAN O'BRIEN

66

I was selfish before.
Everyone is. But when you
have kids, they become
your main priority.

DAVID BECKHAM

99

IT'S THE COURAGE TO RAISE A CHILD THAT MAKES YOU A FATHER.

BARACK OBAMA

Being a great father is
like shaving. No matter
how good you shaved
today, you have to do
it again tomorrow.

REED MARKHAM

THERE'S NO PILLOW

QUITE SO SOFT

AS A FATHER'S

STRONG SHOULDER.

RICHARD L. EVANS

Raising kids is part joy and
part guerrilla warfare.

ED ASNER

DAD TO THE RESCUE!

"

My father didn't tell me
how to live; he lived, and
let me watch him do it.

CLARENCE BUDINGTON KELLAND

"

When I was a kid, I used to imagine animals running under my bed. I told my dad... He cut the legs off the bed.

LOU BROCK

Of all the titles I've been privileged to have, "Dad" has always been the best.

KEN NORTON

I WOULD WANT MY

LEGACY TO BE THAT

I WAS A GREAT SON,

FATHER AND FRIEND.

DANTE HALL

Character is largely caught, and the father and the home should be the great sources of character infection.

FRANK H. CHELEY

Dads are most ordinary men turned by love into heroes, adventurers, story-tellers, and singers of song.

PAM BROWN

"

It's only when you grow up
and take a step back from
him... it's only then that you
can measure his greatness
and fully appreciate it.

MARGARET TRUMAN ON FATHERS

"

EVERYTHING I AM, YOU HELPED ME TO BE.

Dads are stone skimmers, mud wallowers, water wallopers, ceiling swoopers, shoulder gallopers, upsy-downsy, over-and-through, round-and-about whooshers.

HELEN THOMSON

> I am not ashamed to say that no man I ever met was my father's equal, and I never loved any other man as much.

HEDY LAMARR

IT'S BEEN THE MOST

AMAZING EXPERIENCE

I COULD EVER

POSSIBLY IMAGINE.

HARRY, DUKE OF SUSSEX
ON BECOMING A DAD

[My dad] never stopped working to make sure we had the best life possible.

CHRISSY TEIGEN

It is amazing how quickly the kids learn to drive a car, yet are unable to understand the lawnmower... or vacuum cleaner.

BEN BERGOR

A FAMILY NEEDS A FATHER TO ANCHOR IT.

L. TOM PERRY

> An almost perfect relationship with his father was the earthly root of all his wisdom.

C. S. LEWIS

YOU INSPIRE ME TO WORK HARD AND FOLLOW MY DREAMS.

WE LOOKED UP TO OUR

FATHER. HE STILL IS

MUCH GREATER THAN US.

WYNTON MARSALIS

IT IS A WISE FATHER THAT KNOWS HIS CHILD.

WILLIAM SHAKESPEARE

Start children off on the way they should go, and even when they are old they will not turn from it.

PROVERBS 22:6

> I believe that what we become depends on what our fathers teach us... We are formed by little scraps of wisdom.

UMBERTO ECO

I'm looking at [my daughter] right now. To think that I am her dad is the greatest honour in the world.

HARRY CONNICK JR

MY FATHER'S BUSY
BUT HE ALWAYS
HAS TIME FOR ME.

JUDY BLUME

You don't raise heroes, you raise sons. And if you treat them like sons, they'll turn out to be heroes.

WALTER M. SCHIRRA SR

I AM SO GRATEFUL FOR ALL YOU'VE DONE FOR ME.

THE SOONER YOU TREAT

YOUR SON AS A MAN, THE

SOONER HE WILL BE ONE.

JOHN DRYDEN

> Each day of our lives we make deposits in the memory banks of our children.

CHARLES R. SWINDOLL

BEING A FATHER IS THE SINGLE GREATEST FEELING ON EARTH.

RYAN REYNOLDS

THE FAMILY IS ONE
OF NATURE'S
MASTERPIECES.

GEORGE SANTAYANA

My dad. One of the wisest, most authentic, integrity filled, heartful people I've ever known. He shaped me into who I am.

CONNIE BRITTON

A father is someone
you look up to
no matter how
tall you grow.

ANONYMOUS

THERE'S NOTHING THAT

MAKES YOU MORE

INSANE THAN FAMILY.

OR MORE HAPPY.

JIM BUTCHER

I AM A BETTER
PERSON BECAUSE
OF YOU.

THE RAISING OF A

CHILD IS THE BUILDING

OF A CATHEDRAL.

YOU CAN'T CUT CORNERS.

DAVE EGGERS

"

Anyone who tells you
fatherhood is the greatest
thing that can happen to you,
they are understating it.

MIKE MYERS

"

Being a father has
been, without a doubt,
my greatest source of
achievement, pride
and inspiration.

NAVEEN JAIN

OLD AS SHE
WAS, SHE
STILL MISSED
HER DADDY
SOMETIMES.

GLORIA NAYLOR

BEING A FATHER,

BEING A FRIEND,

THOSE ARE THE THINGS

THAT MAKE ME

FEEL SUCCESSFUL.

WILLIAM HURT

TO HER, THE
NAME OF FATHER
WAS ANOTHER
NAME FOR LOVE.

FANNY FERN

Father, Dad, Papa,
no matter what you call
them they influence our
lives and they are the
person we look up to.

CATHERINE PULSIFER

I AM PROUD TO CALL YOU MY DAD.

My father, he was like the rock, the guy you went to with every problem.

GWYNETH PALTROW

WHEN MY FATHER
DIDN'T HAVE MY HAND,
HE HAD MY BACK.

LINDA POINDEXTER

"

Having children is like living in a frat house. Nobody sleeps, everything's broken, and there's a lot of throwing up.

RAY ROMANO

By the time a man realizes that maybe his father was right, he usually has a son who thinks he's wrong.

CHARLES WADSWORTH

> My father gave me the greatest gift anyone could give another person: he believed in me.

JIM VALVANO

A FATHER MAINTAINS

TEN CHILDREN BETTER

THAN TEN CHILDREN

[MAINTAIN] ONE FATHER.

GERMAN PROVERB

Children have never been
very good at listening to
their elders, but they have
never failed to imitate them.

JAMES BALDWIN

"

A father's solemn duty is
to watch football with his
children and teach them
when to shout at the ref.

PAUL COLLINS

Always kiss your children goodnight, even if they're already asleep.

H. JACKSON BROWN JR

IT IS NOT FLESH AND BLOOD, BUT THE HEART WHICH MAKES US FATHERS AND SONS.

JOHANN FRIEDRICH VON SCHILLER

YOU'RE
MORE THAN
MY FATHER
- YOU'RE MY
FRIEND.

Sometimes the poorest man leaves his children the richest inheritance.

RUTH E. RENKEL

IF YOUR CHILDREN LOOK

UP TO YOU, YOU'VE

MADE A SUCCESS OF

LIFE'S BIGGEST JOB.

ANONYMOUS

It has given me purpose, taught me patience, and expanded my heart.

NEIL PATRICK HARRIS ON FATHERHOOD

MY FATHER
HAD A PROFOUND
INFLUENCE ON
ME – HE WAS
A LUNATIC.

SPIKE MILLIGAN

YOU KNOW ME
BETTER THAN
ANYONE.

> My mother gave me
> my drive, but my father
> gave me my dreams.

LIZA MINNELLI

I cannot think of any need in childhood as strong as the need for a father's protection.

SIGMUND FREUD

HOW SWEET 'TIS TO SIT 'NEATH A FOND FATHER'S SMILE.

JOHN HOWARD PAYNE

My dad is truly the best. He is everything a father should be and the greatest man I will ever know.

DAKOTA FANNING

YOU WILL
ALWAYS BE
YOUR CHILD'S
FAVOURITE
TOY.

VICKI LANSKY

SLEEP IS NON-EXISTENT.

IT'S CHAOS AT TIMES,

BUT THERE'S SUCH

JOY IN THE HOUSE.

BRAD PITT

[DAD] OPENED
THE JAR OF PICKLES
WHEN NO ONE
ELSE COULD.

ERMA BOMBECK

FAMILY IS NOT AN

IMPORTANT THING.

IT'S EVERYTHING.

MICHAEL J. FOX

THE SECRET OF FATHERHOOD IS TO KNOW WHEN TO STOP TICKLING.

ANONYMOUS

I DEFINITELY DON'T
TELL YOU ENOUGH
HOW MUCH YOU
MEAN TO ME.

Father! – to God himself we cannot give a holier name.

WILLIAM WORDSWORTH

There's nothing more contagious than the dignity of a father.

AMIT RAY

"

Your children need your presence
more than your presents.

JESSE JACKSON

I haven't taught people in 50 years what my father taught by example in one week.

MARIO CUOMO

IT WAS MY FATHER
WHO TAUGHT ME
TO VALUE MYSELF.

DAWN FRENCH

YOU'RE ALWAYS AROUND WHEN I NEED YOU.

Be kind to thy father, for
when thou wert young, who
loved thee so fondly as he?

MARGARET ANN COURTNEY

MY DAD'S PANTS KEPT

CREEPING UP ON HIM.

BY 65 HE WAS JUST

A PAIR OF PANTS

AND A HEAD.

JEFF ALTMAN

Most of the time I feel
entirely unqualified to
be a parent. I call these
times being awake.

JIM GAFFIGAN

My father was very important to me, because he made me think.

JANIS JOPLIN

"

I think my dad is a lot
cooler than other dads.
He still acts like he's 17.

MILEY CYRUS

"

FATHER OF FATHERS,

MAKE ME ONE,

A FIT EXAMPLE

FOR A SON.

DOUGLAS MALLOCH

Well, it's hard to know
what to get the man who
provides everything.

**MICHAEL FELDMAN
ON RECEIVING A SET OF HOSE
NOZZLES ON FATHER'S DAY**

I SMILE BECAUSE YOU'RE MY FATHER. I LAUGH BECAUSE THERE'S NOTHING YOU CAN DO ABOUT IT.

LIFE DOESN'T COME WITH AN INSTRUCTION BOOK. THAT'S WHY WE HAVE FATHERS.

H. JACKSON BROWN JR

"

There is a special place in
heaven for the father who
takes his daughter shopping.

JOHN SINOR

"

A HAPPY FAMILY IS BUT AN EARLIER HEAVEN.

GEORGE BERNARD SHAW

I DON'T MIND LOOKING

IN THE MIRROR AND

SEEING MY FATHER.

MICHAEL DOUGLAS

If you ever want to torture my dad, tie him up and right in front of him, refold a map incorrectly.

CATHY LADMAN

Families are the compass that guides us.

BRAD HENRY

"

I've never slept less and dealt with more poop and been so excited about it!

JUSTIN TIMBERLAKE ON BECOMING A DAD

"

THERE'S NOTHING LIKE AN ADVENTURE WITH DAD.

HAVING ONE CHILD

MAKES YOU A PARENT;

HAVING TWO,

YOU ARE A REFEREE.

DAVID FROST

THERE IS
NO JOB
MORE
IMPORTANT
THAN
PARENTING.

BEN CARSON

**NOBLE
FATHERS HAVE
NOBLE CHILDREN.**

EURIPIDES

He was a father.
That's what a father
does. Eases the burdens
of those he loves.

GEORGE SAUNDERS

"

A father's smile has been known
to light up a child's entire day.

SUSAN GALE

"

As I've gotten older,
I've realized my true
models are my parents...
My dad is so strong.

ZENDAYA

MY DAUGHTER GOT ME

A "WORLD'S BEST DAD"

MUG. SO WE KNOW

SHE'S SARCASTIC.

BOB ODENKIRK

IF AT FIRST YOU DON'T SUCCEED, CALL DAD!

When I was twenty-something, I asked my father, "When did you start feeling like a grown-up?" His response: "Never".

SHANNON CELEBI

THERE IS MORE TO FATHERS THAN MEETS THE EYE.

MARGARET ATWOOD

IT ISN'T
THE SIZE OF
THE FAMILY,
IT'S THE
INTERACTIONS
OF THE
MEMBERS
INSIDE.

MICHELE BORBA

Setting a good example for children takes all the fun out of middle age.

WILLIAM FEATHER

Being a dad is more
important than football,
more important
than anything.

DAVID BECKHAM

CHILDREN LEARN TO SMILE FROM THEIR PARENTS.

SHINICHI SUZUKI

I realized being a father
is the greatest job I have
ever had and the greatest
job I will ever have.

DWAYNE JOHNSON

I WILL NEVER GROW TOO OLD FOR A HUG.

"

My father is my rock. It's where I learned everything about loyalty, dependability, being there day in, day out, no matter what.

HUGH JACKMAN

WHAT DO I OWE MY FATHER? EVERYTHING.

HENRY VAN DYKE

THE HEART OF A FATHER

IS A MASTERPIECE

OF NATURE.

ANTOINE FRANÇOIS
PRÉVOST D'EXILES

LATELY, ALL MY FRIENDS ARE WORRIED THAT THEY'RE TURNING INTO THEIR FATHERS. I'M WORRIED THAT I'M NOT.

DAN ZEVIN

Dad always called me his "favourite son".

CAMERON DIAZ
ON BEING A TOMBOY

I EVEN LAUGH AT YOUR DAD JOKES.

I'm looking out for myself, but I'm looking out for my dad, too.

JAMIE REDKNAPP

> A daughter needs a dad to be the standard against which she will judge all men.

GREGORY E. LANG

A FATHER IS A BANKER

PROVIDED BY NATURE.

FRENCH PROVERB

I have found the very
best way to give advice
to your children is to find
out what they want and
then advise them to do it.

HARRY S. TRUMAN

Nothing could get at me if I curled up on my father's lap... All about him was safe.

NAOMI MITCHISON

FATHERHOOD IS THE GREATEST THING THAT COULD EVER HAPPEN.

MICHAEL BUBLÉ

MY DAD IS MY HERO.

> The most extraordinary thing about having a child is people think I'm a responsible human being.

COLIN FARRELL

THE MOST IMPORTANT

THING IN THE WORLD

IS FAMILY AND LOVE.

JOHN WOODEN

My dad is a hero. I'm never free of a problem, nor do I truly experience joy until we share it.

NANCY SINATRA

Having a kid is like falling in love for the first time when you're 12, but every day.

MIKE MYERS

A father is a man who
expects his son to
be as good a man as
he meant to be.

FRANK A. CLARK

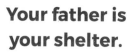

**Your father is
your shelter.**

ANONYMOUS

ONE FATHER IS MORE

THAN A HUNDRED

SCHOOLMASTERS.

GEORGE HERBERT

YOU'RE TOTALLY RAD, DAD.

IN TIME OF TEST, FAMILY IS BEST.

BURMESE PROVERB

> Every son's first superhero is his father, and it was the same for me. For me, he was Superman and Batman combined.

TIGER SHROFF

OF ALL THE ROCKS UPON WHICH WE BUILD OUR LIVES... FAMILY IS THE MOST IMPORTANT.

BARACK OBAMA

DAD HUGS ARE THE BEST HUGS.

"

A child looks up at the stars
and wonders. A great father
puts a child on his shoulders
and helps them to grab a star.

REED MARKHAM

"

PARENTHOOD
REMAINS THE
GREATEST
SINGLE
PRESERVE
OF THE
AMATEUR.

ALVIN TOFFLER

A FATHER IS THE ONE

FRIEND UPON WHOM

WE CAN ALWAYS RELY.

ÉMILE GABORIAU

YOU'RE THE BEST
DAD EVER!

If you're interested in finding out more about our books, find us on Facebook at **Summersdale Publishers** and follow us on Twitter at @Summersdale.

www.summersdale.com